Insights from the Underside

Insights from the Underside

An Intergenerational Conversation of Ministers

■

Edited by

Neal D. Presa

BROADMIND PRESS

Elizabeth, NJ

Published by Broadmind Press
an imprint of Hollym International Corp.
www.broadmindpress.com

ISBN: 978-1-56591-357-8
Library of Congress Control Number: 2007943229

Cover design by TurnThru Creative
www.turnthru.com

Manufactured in the United States of America

*To the great cloud of witnesses
from generation to generation,
then, now, and in the years to come*

Table of Contents

Appendices

About the Contributors

Craig Barnes is senior pastor of Shadyside Presbyterian Church and the Robert Meneilly Professor of Pastoral Ministry at Pittsburgh Theological Seminary.

John T. Galloway, Jr. is the retired senior pastor of Wayne Presbyterian Church in Wayne, PA.

Thomas W. Gillespie is president and professor of New Testament emeritus of Princeton Theological Seminary (1983-2004).

William "Bill" A.C. Golderer is convening minister of the Broad Street Ministry in Philadelphia, PA.

Jud Hendrix is the co-organizing pastor of Covenant Community Church in Louisville, KY.

Deborah van deusen Hunsinger is professor of pastoral theology at Princeton Theological Seminary.

Elizabeth "Liz" Kaznak is co-organizing pastor of Covenant Community Church in Louisville, KY.

Hope Italiano Lee is pastor of Valley Forge Presbyterian Church in King of Prussia, PA and a DMin candidate in homiletics at Gordon Conwell Theological Seminary.

Sung Lee is associate pastor for youth at Lower Providence Presbyterian Church in Eagleville, PA.

Laura S. Mendenhall is president of Columbia Theological Seminary.

Rodger Nishioka is associate professor of Christian Education at Columbia Theological Seminary and a PhD candidate at Georgia State University.

Lonnie Oliver is pastor of New Life Presbyterian Church in College Park, GA, and was most recently a member of the Theological Task Force on Peace, Unity, and Purity.

Neal D. Presa is pastor of Middlesex Presbyterian Church in Middlesex, NJ and a PhD candidate in liturgical studies at Drew University.

Bruce Reyes Chow is organizing pastor of the Mission Bay Community Church in San Francisco, CA. He is a candidate for Moderator of the 218th General Assembly (2008) of the Presbyterian Church (U.S.A.).

David Shinn is associate pastor for parish life at Plymouth Congregational Church in Seattle, WA.

Mienda Uriarte was coordinator for youth and young adult ministries for the Congregational Ministries Division, General Assembly Council (2001-2006) and is a DMin candidate in executive leadership at McCormick Theological Seminary.

Steve Toshio Yamaguchi is executive presbyter of the Presbytery of Los Ranchos.

Foreword

Keepin' On, Keepin' On

At Columbia Theological Seminary, where I am privileged to serve on the faculty, there is a friend of mine named Alexander Oliver. Mr. Oliver is part of our maintenance crew and has been around for some time. Once when I asked how long he had been at Columbia, he replied looking down as he often does when he is talking to you, "Long time." When I asked how long, he sighed and said, "Professor, I'm old." When I asked how old, he thought for a while, smiled and then said with a chuckle, "Older than dirt." That's pretty old. A highlight of the year is when Mr. Oliver is coaxed to sing in a chapel service. Word spreads quickly that Mr. Oliver is going to sing and the chapel gets full. He comes in wearing his uniform and in our chapel, so quiet it seems as if we are holding our collective breaths, he begins to line out a spiritual that is no doubt lodged deep in his bones. For instance, I thought I knew the song "Wade in the Water" but quite honestly when I first heard Mr. Oliver sing it, I realized then and there that I had never heard the song before. He is a handsome, if ancient, black man who for some reason has taken a liking to this, his first "oriental" friend as he reminds me.

Whenever I see Mr. Oliver, I ask how he is doing and more often than not, he says, in his quiet way, "Oh, you know professor, keepin' on, keepin' on." To parse that phrase, I would say it means persevering much like the idea in Hebrews 12:1 about "run[ning] with perseverance the race set before us." It seems to me that Mr. Oliver is reminding me of the wisdom and the challenge before many in ministry these days … the task of keepin' on, keepin' on.

The task of ministry is, as the writer to the Hebrews reminds us, a challenge. It is running the race with perseverance. It is the long stretch after the excitement at the start of the race and well before the thrill at the end of it. It is the idea of constancy and consistency. It is the idea of abiding when in John 15 Jesus calls upon us to "abide in me as I abide in you." It is remaining. It is staying. It is hanging in there and doing the routine and going through the motions not because it thrills us but because we called to it. This is a contrary idea, I realize, today, in this age of instant gratification and consumerism and extreme sports and thrill-a-minute adventures but the truth is that ministry is going to take time.

It seems to me that much of what we are struggling with in ministry today is the dominant narrative of the romantic hermeneutic that tells us that every single moment of ministry, every conversation, every interaction is to be both productive and fulfilling and dramatic and life changing. It simply is not nor can it be true.

The challenge is to keep on keepin' on and to not subscribe to the romantic notions of ministry that surround us and ultimately disable us. Romantic notions can get in the way. We must come to grips with the positivist tapes playing in our heads and reinforced in our culture that everything we do has to be an emotional high and must result in something that is tangible and immediate and can be quantified or our work is for not. I am reminded that it is part of the rhythm of life that not all of our Sundays are high holy days like Christmas and Easter and Pentecost and that is why the ecclesial calendar is filled with 33, count them, 33 Sundays in "ordinary time." Virtually eight months of the year are designated Sundays in ordinary time. To be sure, ordinary time does not mean stagnant time. In fact, the days of ordinary time are to be marked by continuing growth, but these days are separated from the high holy days and they are in the vast majority by a ratio of 2:1. These are the days of constancy and consistency—the days of keepin' on, keepin' on.

iv

Keepin' on, keepin' on challenges the dominant narrative that ministry must always be thrilling and fulfilling or it is not ministry at all.

This book you hold is about all of this: constancy and consistency, perseverance in ministry, managing to live faithfully even in the days of ordinary time. It is a collection of testimonies from those who are newer on the road of ministry with follow up thoughtful reflections from those who are farther down the road. It is invaluable in that it bears potent witness to Christ's call to persevere. For all of us, I believe we are called to constancy and perseverance as a means of grace in our own lives and in the lives of others and ultimately as a point of entry into the world so that holy vibrations are created that radiate far beyond the church. To be sure, perseverance is not easy. Perseverance is not always fun. But it is the journey to which we have been called.

Toward the end of J.R.R. Tolkein's book, *Two Towers*, he writes of a conversation between two travelers, the hobbits Sam and Frodo:

> "I don't like anything here at all," said Frodo, "step or stone, breath or bone. Earth, air and water all seem accursed. But so our path is laid."

> "Yes, that's so," said Sam. "And we shouldn't be here at all, if we'd known more about it before we started. But I supposed it's often that way. The brave things in the old tales and songs, Mr. Frodo, adventures, as I used to call them. I used to think that they were things the wonderful folk of the stories went out and looked for, because they wanted them, because they were exciting and life was a bit dull, a kind of sport, as you might say. But that's not the way of it with the tales that really mattered, or the ones that stay in the mind.

Folk seem to have been just landed in them, usually—their paths were laid that way, as you put it. But I expect they had lots of chances, like us, of turning back, only they didn't. And if they had, we shouldn't know, because they'd have been forgotten. We only hear about those as just went on."

That is so much of the journey of ministry. Not necessarily seeking it out but just landing in it because one's path has been laid. And it's not turning back despite numerous opportunities to do so. The journeys we hear about, the tales worth telling, are all about those who just went on.

How are you doing today, Mr. Oliver? Keepin' on, keepin' on. Thanks be to God.

Rodger Nishioka
Columbia Theological Seminary
Decatur, GA

Editor's Preface:
Why This Book and Why Now?

In the summer of 2002, the former Office of Youth and Young Ministries, Presbyterian Church (U.S.A.), convened a meeting of 16 young adult ministry practitioners at the Montreat Conference Center in order to envision the contours of ministry by and with young adults in the Church and world today, and to provide encouragement and support for the journey of faith and service. The method? We were instructed to draft papers, present them in front of the group, then field any question imaginable. While it felt like a seminar at an academic conference, the result was a free-flow sharing of the heart and mind, honesty about our vulnerabilities and strengths, and, what I called then, a genesis of a "mini-revolution" and modern-day reformation of what it means to be the Church of Jesus Christ in today's space and time.

My generation of ministers serves at a time unlike any other that the Christian Church has seen. Information and digital technology, 9/11 and the war on terrorism, an evenly divided American electorate of Blue states and Red States, and a very spiritual, but not necessarily Christian nation are core features of the society and culture within which we live, study, raise our families, teach, minister, witness, pray, worship, and be. It's not that our time is any more complicated than the first century church as it tried to grapple with its own identity within a cultural and religious landscape that were likewise ever-changing and unfamiliar, particularly as the demands of being the people of the Way necessitated a new way of thinking and living. Each period of history presents its own complexities and challenges. But our time, the beginning of the 21st century, presents some unique challenges that the world and the Church have not experienced, while still confronting the same ones of previous generations. Religious pluralism now, particularly after 9/11, is no more complicated than it was during the apostle Paul's day. Read the book of James and the apostle's epistles to Corinth and Galatia for a broad stroke treatment of religious pluralism and difference.

But, our context requires a reassessment of what we have inherited, where we are at, and what lies ahead. This book affirms the diachronic (across time) nature of ministry challenges, but lifts up the synchronic (with the present time) character of challenges unique to 21st century living. The stories that unfold in this book are a humble attempt at an intergenerational dialogue about the crucial matters of faith, vocation, and life. In it are the reflections and recollections, the hopes and prayers, the lessons learned and the lessons imparted of young adult ministers (under the age of 40) and more "seasoned" veteran ministers. Together, the 18 contributors to this book bring almost 350 years of service to ministry, serving in congregations, seminaries, middle-governing bodies, and specialized ministries.

But, ordained ministry is not our only, and not even our primary, vocation. What does it mean to serve faithfully as a disciple of Jesus Christ today? Our vocation as Christ's disciples includes ordained ministry, but not exclusively. As Christ's disciples we are to live faithfully in all of our relationships— spouse, parent, friend, caregiver—just as much as all the other "functions" and "identities" of being an ordained officer in the church: pastor, shepherd, teacher, evangelist, executive presbyter, seminary president, community activist, administrator, professor, Eucharistic presider, preacher, the baptized. This is what we bring. Each of us bring to the discussion table our various roles, identities, and callings. How can we do otherwise? For in any given day or any given moment, we are tasked to live out each of those separate callings at home, church, the public square, in our families. How well we negotiate those roles and identities in those contexts and in the context of the Church and world today will largely determine the difference between the minister who thrives and the minister who merely survives.

This book harnesses the rich diversity—theological, racial-ethnic, geographical, experiential, educational, age—that make up the Presbyterian Church (U.S.A.). Each writer puts theology and life to pen, writing in their own unique style— some more academic in prose, others more poetic or conversational. Our intent: to describe what we have experienced, learned, practiced, and lived through our various vocations in the church study, in the pulpit, in a theological seminary, raising our children, walking down the marriage aisle, receiving the laying on of hands by fellow presbyters, managing conflict in session meetings, speaking from our knees. This is no less than the on-going story of all generation of ministers past and present, and a look at how we can do even better in the craft called *vocation*. Let the church-wide conversations begin!

To all my friends and colleagues who wrote for this project, I am grateful for your contribution to this book and for receiving my continual, friendly nudgings in the last three years. I am hopeful that this little volume will help many in our beloved Church—pastors, professors, governing body officials, specialized ministers, seminary administrators, committees on preparation for ministry, committees on ministry, and inquirers and candidates for the ordained ministry—find their story in our stories or add theirs to ours, as we have been called into the story of Jesus Christ's servant life, death, and resurrection.

The community of Middlesex Presbyterian Church (MPC), with whom I am honored to serve as pastor, deserves special mention. We have been patient with each other, and continue to learn from each other. The Session and members of MPC provided me the latitude to work on this project.

To our good friend, David Yun, principal of TurnThru Creative, who generously provided services in developing the Broadmind Press logo and book cover. You are too cool!

Finally, I am ever so grateful to my family: my sons, Daniel and Andrew, who had to wait for daddy to play trains while I was working on this project; and last but certainly not least, my beloved and patient wife, Grace, who held the fort of our home as I worked and who heard every mutation of this project since its genesis through its completion. I love the three of you so very much! *Soli Deo gloria.*

Neal D. Presa, *Editor*
Middlesex, NJ
Advent 2007

I

Location, Location, Location:
Ministry and Living in the 21st Century

Bruce Reyes-Chow

Is context really everything? This is the ultimate postmodern 21st century question that many of our congregations have been struggling with as of late. The postmodern debate over the importance of context, one that frames ministry around a community's particular worldview, life experiences and commonalities, is a question that I too wrestle with daily. As a pastor of one of those funky new "Postmodern" and "Emergent" congregations, I have come to the realization that for one to pastor/lead/influence a vital, thriving church community today, one *must* understand and embrace the context in which one serves.

First, as appropriate, let me set my own context—a.k.a. "the postmodern disclaimer"—both in my approach to ministry and my specific context.

As I muse on the concept of context I am only speaking from my own experience. This is not a cop-out as some would like to think, but shared with the knowledge that others may find places where we are similar as well as areas that we are clearly different. I operate with the understanding that there are no "one size fits all" answers, but by the sharing and reflecting upon one another's experiences we will each be helped in our personal discernment of what God hopes for each of us. Also, while I am trying to disguise myself as a deep thinking, theologically profound advocate of grace-filled transformation, I am really just a practitioner trying to find a way to be a faithful

1

servant of God in a world that seems increasingly chaotic and down-right crazy.

I currently serve as the pastor of a new church development in San Francisco that is intentionally focused on the lives of the city's new "Urbanites." We have been around for about five years and have experienced both the extravagances and excitement of the *dot.com* boom as well as the struggles and despair of the *dot.com* bust. We are extremely transient, turning over at least two or three times during our young life. We have met in seven locations, from churches to homes to cafés. We are socio-economically middle- to upper-middle class, about 40% White, 40% Asian American and 20% other, educated and slightly left-of- center theologically and politically. We could be described by any and all of the latest terminology for this kind of community: "Postmodern," "Emergent," "BoBo," "Cultural Creative," etc. We are about sixty or so on Sundays with all but about four folks under forty. Services are filled with an urban jazz musicality fully embracing an emergent and Reformed form of worship. The common bond is a yearning to be connected to God in a way that is meaningful and relevant in the surrounding world of chaos that is opposed to such a community.

As I think about its importance, I have begun to appreciate context in a new way. I was raised in a church that always worked against the "Sunday is the most segregated day in the U.S." reality. This posture always raised great tensions for me as I was also raised in a denomination that valued gathering in ethnic congregations. My denomination, progressive as it is, has always seemed to have this schizophrenic posture of wanting to be "multicultural" while supporting affinity-based congregations (based on age, ethnicity, etc.) for the furthering of the Gospel. I know there is an inherent and justified fear of becoming exclusive, but as I have been serving a rather homogenous community, I would ask the question, "Is homogeneity always bad?"

My first response would be, surely the "H" word can't be good. And yes, while taken to an extreme and used as a tool for exclusion, it is bad, wrong, ugly, etc., but when healthy, I believe the realities of a "Healthy Homogeneity" can actually help us to create stronger local congregations and in turn a stronger larger church. Hasn't this been the point of ethnic-based congregations all along: understand context, build around affinity and strengthen the larger church?

When it comes to building up the larger church, I think we can learn a great deal from this ethnic-based congregational methodology. I also believe, however, that we should push this question out a little further beyond ethnic-based congregations. In today's culture, if our churches are going to not just survive but thrive, we must work towards understanding our context so we can reach the point of having what I would call a "Healthy Homogeneity."

First, let me set the parameters and some assumptions that I am making as I propose this idea of a "Healthy Homogeneity."

▸ *I am only talking about the local congregation.* Although the church at the denominational level clearly has its own forms of homogeneity, it is the larger gathering of these smaller communities that creates a fuller image of creation. Ethnic-based congregations create a more complete picture of the Kingdom of God, and congregations of like theology, age, style, setting, etc. can do the same.

▸ *I am not only talking about racial homogeneity.* There can be a healthy homogeneity of socio-economics, class, age, church experience, life situation, theological perspective, family structure, and the like. In many ways, ethnic homogeneity is easier to differentiate than other types; it

3

is visible in faces, food, and common practices. Other types of homogeneity may not be as easily identified.

▸ *I am taking seriously the reality that many have been excluded from the church but yearn for a place to connect with God.* The reality is that some groups of people have been left out of the embrace of the church, and a community built around a Healthy Homogeneity has great potential to be a place for more folks to experience the transformative life in Christ.

With these assumptions in mind, here is what I think characterizes a congregation that understands its context well enough to develop a Healthy Homogeneity:

▸ *It understands Homogeneity as a natural part of being community.* One of the biggest mistakes that the church has made is to fight against the natural inclination for human beings to gather with like human beings. Whether it is age, gender, class, theology, etc., there is comfort when people can gather with and share "unspoken" stories. Often these stories concern shared experiences of pain and exclusion. Healing can happen most effectively in the context of others who have had similar experiences. *Every* church is gathered around some kind of homogeneity; whether we acknowledge it or not. While there are certainly dangers inherent in homogeneous communities, at their most natural and best they provide safe places for challenge and transformation to happen.

▸ *It understands its homogeny, both its joys as well as its pitfalls.* While a natural part of the human condition, homogeneity can easily turn a community to a posture of exclusion rather than embrace. The greatest danger of homogeneity is the temptation for folks to worship it as though it is a god to be worshiped and served rather than a condition of commonality that draws people together to worship and serve God. If a congregation understands this real danger, it will be able to make intentional choices in its life that focus around celebrating its owned commonalities rather than focusing on who does not belong. It is a fine and subtle line, but one that ethnic churches have lived out for generations. Congregations can lift up commonalities without inherently being exclusive.

▶ *It intentionally finds ways to move outside of its particular homogeneity.* If a congregation is going to be part of the larger kingdom and avoid becoming insular and irrelevant, it must be intentional about experiencing life and ministry beyond its inherent comfort zones. A congregation that understands this will be secure enough to step out of its norm and see its place in the larger church and Kingdom. Homogeneity is not the goal but a valid gathering point and place of rejuvenation from which we are sent into the world.

▶ *It embraces its homogeneity in a way that allows folks to connect with the complex comfort, challenge, and mystery of Christ.* This is the most important trait of a Healthy Homogeneity in that it takes seriously how people connect with God and how God may be active in their lives. In this respect a Healthy Homogeneity provides a situation ripe for folks to experience at least three things:

1. *Comfort of God:* In the context where I serve, the folks who are part of this community were (un)intentionally excluded by the church for years. Without any kind of meaningful relationship with

5

the church, many of these folks have felt greatly misunderstood and chastised for their actions, politics, and spirituality among other things. Whether through the subtleties of style, structure, technology or dogma, many have felt abandoned and ignored by the church. And yet despite all this, they still yearn for some connection to God through the church. These are folks who have moved from thinking that they can be Christians in isolation to committing to being part of a community grounded together in Christ. Our homogeneity provides a foundation of love and security that makes room for the challenges that a life in Christ can bring.

2. *Challenges of Christ:* A Healthy Homogeneity does not mean coddling or the creation of an "everybody-be-happy" social club. It is in fact quite the opposite; the comfort that is created is simply a means to remind folks that in the midst of great transformation, God is and will always be present. In my context, there is great challenge around economic and class issues as well as personal relationships. Folks are constantly being challenged about how we use our wealth, power and privilege, about personal relationships, and how we interact with the "other" in our midst. By knowing that certain parts of our life and journey are understood and embraced, we are more willing and able to be open to the possibility of transformation in other parts of our life.

3. *Mystery of the Faith:* As a pastor of a church that understands its homogeneity I am free to help folks experience the mysteries of God in both specific and general ways. From knowing the capacity of people to experience worship through multiple media

experiences, to embracing healthy ways of electronic communication to build community, understanding where folks are coming from allows me to be a more effective guide for them on their spiritual walk.

I obviously think context is important, but "everything" it is not. Just as any part of one's ministry can be lifted up to become an idol, understanding context is not the be-all and end-all of ministry. The "everything" for me is the goal of creating communities where people can experience Christ in all the wonderful and challenging ways that God has made possible. In the movement towards that end, while not everything, acknowledging and understanding context is pretty important.

Response by Craig Barnes
to Bruce Reyes-Chow on Context

It makes sense, I suppose. If you take context seriously, and define it by a targeted audience for church growth, then you would end up with a certain amount of homogeneity. And the best you could hope for is what Bruce has advocated—a healthy homogeneity. It makes sense, but I'm still not sure it is all the church is called to be.

Twenty-five years ago, when I was leaving seminary we would have thought that healthy homogeneity was an oxymoron. Diversity is healthy for congregations, we were told. Multiculturalism is healthy. Integration is really healthy. Many of our seminary professors had marched with Dr. King for civil rights, and they couldn't help but instill his dream of a color-blind society into our vision of the local congregation. So much had already been sacrificed by so many. Our job was to keep the dream alive.

There was a school of strategy at that time called the "Church Growth Movement" that advocated homogeneity as an evangelistic technique. More than one of my professors thought it was pretty much a heresy. "The church cannot remain segregated because Christ is not divided," we were told repeatedly. Right. I believed that then, and I still do. But the thing that has always stuck in my craw is that the churches that apply the Church Growth principles typically grow. And after 25 years of hearing about diversity and multiculturalism in the Presbyterian Church, the denomination is still predominately white—maybe whiter than that. And it has been declining in membership at a steady rate.

So to recap: what is wrong seems to be working, and what is right doesn't work. If we were successful at creating multicultural congregations and were still declining in numbers, we could at least feel better about the cost of being "right." But the typical PC(U.S.A.) congregation only talks about diversity to fewer and fewer people in the pews. Presbyterians love to finesse their way out of this dilemma by toying around with definitions. "But what does growth really mean?" And we certainly pride ourselves on having a prophetic message that is unpopular. Maybe, but even dead right is still dead.

Still, I just don't know if I can give up the dream of growing, diverse congregations.

Bruce has taken a huge risk with this essay. He is challenging the now time-honored assumption that every congregation must strive for heterogenic community. The ironies of this coming from an Asian American pastor, who grew up on the vision of transforming Sunday from being "the most segregated day," and who actually has a racially integrated congregation all need to be honored. Clearly, Bruce knows the dream of an ethnically diverse congregation and has seen the dream come true. But he knows it is not enough. That's the problem with the diversity goal—you never accomplish enough. Even if you achieve ethnic diversity then you have to worry about another form, such as generational diversity. Again, ironically, in the case of Bruce's church it was precisely because they strove for generational homogeneity that they were able to achieve ethnic diversity.

His ethnically diverse Emergent congregation lacks old widows who need a ride to church, white haired men who have stood at the doors as ushers for the last thirty course, this also means that Bruce doesn't get sucked into a lot of arguments about the old hymnbook, the Women's Mission Bazaar, or the ugly pulpit that was built by Mrs. Smith's deceased father. But even the absence of those arguments means that his church does not have the generational diversity of those congregations that lack the ethnic diversity of his. So Bruce really is dealing with homogeneity, as he admits. But it is precisely the clearly targeted

9

focus that makes his church attractive to those who find themselves in that target—those who are seeking a community that knows how to address the "yearning to be connected to God in a way that is meaningful and relevant in a world of chaos." Right, that's very hip. But who makes the casseroles?

Recently, while teaching a D. Min. seminar, I asked my three African American students to tell me why it is so hard to gain a substantial percentage of minorities in a predominately white church. Their quick response was to say that it really is not about the style of worship. The problem is that the context is simply wrong for them. Much of the Black experience in our country has been about powerlessness, which means that often the message of Black churches is focused on empowering and renewing hope. This message emerges repeatedly in their sermons and music. But when African Americans come to my church they will hear me preaching about sacrifice and the virtue of powerlessness, which is precisely what those living in the context of the majority culture need to hear. But it isn't exactly kerygmatic for many minorities.

So even in my own congregation it is clear that contextualizing the proclamation makes some form of homogeneous grouping inevitable. And that means that the best the homogeneous congregations can do is to follow Bruce's lead in making homogeneity healthy. Among his many guiding principles for this health, I was most struck by the call to move a community intentionally outside of its homogeneity back into the larger context that often looks different from the "valid gathering point" of a smaller targeted context. Although Bruce doesn't draw out the implications of this, it seems to me that this makes a strong theological case for the connectional church. Perhaps we need to stop thinking of valid gathering points as the church, and apply that term only to the larger, more diverse, expression of the Body of Christ.

The congregation I serve as a pastor has tried intentionally to become more racially integrated, and has even

10

hired an African American associate pastor. But I have serious doubts that we will ever achieve a balance of races. However, we have had wonderful success in partnering with African American congregations in mission, worship, educational experiences, and fellowship. Over time, our Black pastor has led our members into significant relationships with brothers and sisters who do not look like us, and who spend most of their week living in very different contexts. But every Sunday morning we still all huddle together in our different homogeneities.

Every time I see our congregation gathered together with those from an African American congregation for a special worship service or a common dinner in the church basement, I give thanks to God for this fuller glimpse of the Body of Christ.

Still, I dream for more. So it only makes sense to pray, "Thy Kingdom come."

II

A Lesson In Love: Being a Spouse

Sung and Hope Lee

It was the best of times. It was the worst of times. There we were, standing at the altar, before God and all of our family and friends about to embark on the magnificent journey of marriage. For two young seminarians, almost pastors, we thought we had the world on a string. A new marriage, new ministries ... a whole new life was about to begin. We thought we had all the answers about life and ministry. We thought we'd get positive support; nothing but joy and excitement as two fresh pastors began their life together in marriage and ministry. What we received was far from positive and not the least bit encouraging. Some of what we heard was: "Ministry is really tough on a marriage"; "A lot of clergy couples just don't make it"; "You'll be lucky to find calls in the same zip code." The ones who were telling us the realities of married life in today's church were the pastors who'd been out serving the church for years. They were also seminary professors and administrators who had already seen plenty of clergy couples. They were clergy couples or ex-clergy/couples themselves who spoke as though they had some authority on the issue. We thought they were all idiots.

After all, in a time when mainline denominations are seeing a decline in membership, what church wouldn't want a dynamic young pastor, brimming with enthusiasm and energy? Better yet, how about two of them?

Three years post-seminary, we found ourselves barely maintaining a marriage in a situation where one of us had our dream call while the other commuted sixty miles (one way) for a part-time call that, because of distance and being part-time, was far from a dream. We just got to a point where it was time to choose which sacrifices to make.

Should we sacrifice our fairly new marriage? What about our family, particularly our daughter? How about our calls, our vocation? It seemed as though any one of the propositions put us on the losing side of what was supposed to be the rest of our lives.

It brings to mind the story of Abraham and Sarah and their son, Isaac. Abraham is called by God to go out and lead the nations. Abraham's call is also Sarah's call. Their marriage is one of the very few marriages lifted up by name in the scriptures. So, Sarah goes with Abraham and they journey together to a point where they have a child. This is where Abraham's and Sarah's call becomes more complicated: they not only are called to lead a nation, called to be spouses—they are now also called to be parents. A child adds a whole new dimension to things, and now Isaac is thrown into the mix. In the course of Abraham's call, God leads Abraham to Mt. Moriah to sacrifice their only son.

What we often forget about this story is that this sacrifice was not just Abraham's; it was Sarah's as well. They had not only been willing to sacrifice their lives, their own identities for God's calling in life to give birth to a nation, but now they literally had to sacrifice the young life that they had given birth to: Isaac. In the end, as we know, God provided for them both because of their faithfulness and trust in God.

The challenge that faces those who are called to serve the Lord and who are called to be married is to have the faith to believe that God will indeed provide. The key word here is "God." Many presbyteries will not understand the plight of young clergy couples, or they will not want to get involved in a church's call process. Perhaps they will advocate living with the consequences of choosing both to be in ministry and married to another pastor. Not every church will understand, either.

Churches run high risks with married pastors and especially pastors who are married to other pastors. One can't blame them for their hesitation. What if they do call a clergy couple? What happens when they go on vacation or when they both leave at the same time? Of course, what if one gets another call? Then a whole congregation stands on precarious ground as the other one tries to find a call in the same state!

It's worth mentioning here that just as all pastors are not created alike, neither are all congregations. Some congregations are willing to step out in faith, if they really believe that an individual is called to their church, without regard to their marital status. Such is the case with both of the congregations we currently serve. Nonetheless, when it comes to call, ultimately we must look to God to provide individual and cooperative calls for entire families.

Similarly, when it comes to marriage, we must look to God to provide. There is not even a successful shot at marriage, unless God looms large in the big picture. For young pastors, who are also fairly new to marriage, this is exceptionally true. In the span of a few years, we find ourselves as spiritual leaders in the community, counseling others on relationships while trying to grow into our own. The learning curve is steep, fast, and can be extremely costly, if not tended to on a regular basis.

The temptation to immerse ourselves in the needs of our congregants often gives us a great excuse not to deal with our own marital issues and needs. It's much easier to discuss Mr. So-and-So's affair than to vent our frustration about the dishes in the kitchen sink that are permanently stuck to one another.

Clergy couples must not fail to set clear boundaries. By the same token, churches must show grace towards those boundaries. Clergy couples must elevate those boundaries to the highest possible degree. This takes hard work. What will you talk about at dinner? How will you spend your weekends? Does the church potluck dinner count as a date?

Frank and open discussions about these and other life and ministry questions must be addressed on a continuing basis. Couples must clearly define their time together because a failure to do so will easily let the church calendar (or calendars) dictate the ebb and flow of life.

Also, it's important to know one's call: one's call to ministry and one's call to family. As members of a clergy couple, each of us sees our call from God as minister, spouse, and parent as exactly that: calls from God. Because we value the calls, we try to the best of our ability to balance our schedules to be faithful to that which God has called us, and with which God has blessed us. Faithfulness involves prioritizing our passions, knowing our strengths and limitations, and understanding that it's not only about ourselves and our own goals but also about the other life with which God has blessed us. Ultimately, faithfulness is the choices we make in daily life, balancing the needs of the church with the needs of our family. We view the needs of our family and our relationship with each other as more fundamental than our call as pastors. As Paul writes concerning church leaders in his first letter to Timothy, if we cannot meet the needs of our own family, it would be ridiculous to think that we might even attempt to meet the needs of our churches. Our goal has always been to try and spend four evenings together and three with the church. That way, we'd never look back and feel that we spent more time with the church than we did with our family. It's a lofty goal. Some weeks we make it and some weeks we do not. But, we try hard to be intentional and to show ourselves a little bit of grace.

There are a few things we have found helpful to keep in mind while in thinking about marriage and what that means for a life in ministry.

First, it's important to remember that marriage is a three-way commitment—a mutual commitment of two people to one another as well as a commitment to God. God must take a central place in marriage. Pray together. Spend time in the Word together. And on those rare occasions (which can be particularly rare for clergy couples who serve different churches), find every opportunity to worship together.

Second, be willing to be creative. Creativity is virtually a necessity for clergy couples. The reality is that both of you may not be able to serve churches. One may have to go into specialized ministry. One may have to consider tent-making. One may end up considering further education. But, we have found that taking turns with calls ("if I let you take this call, you let me pick the next one") is not a good idea. This kind of thinking opens the door to resentment and frustration. Instead, consider where God is calling you together in ministry. With patience and prayer, God will be faithful as long as you are open to being creative.

Third, it is important for all clergy, but particularly young clergy, to be very proactive in the candidating process. Since many young clergy take Associate Pastor positions or solo pastorates in small congregations, it is crucial to be clear about how the Head of Staff or session feel about marriage, family, and ministry. If the pastor or the church is expecting that you will be in the office eighty hours a week with no vacation for the first year, perhaps this is not the best call at this point for your marriage or your ministry. Asking these tough questions on the front end prevents discovering yourself in a precarious situation down the road. And finally, it is crucial to seek out the companionship of others who are sharing your journey. We have found that when we have sought out fellow married and/or clergy couples, each couple thinks their struggles are unique to their marriage. There's no need to suffer in silence. In fact, as clergy couples grow in number it will become more and more important for us to network so that we can be advocates for each other with presbyteries and churches.

Presbyteries and churches also need to start advocating for clergy couples. We live in a world where the institution of marriage is assaulted on a daily basis. Let's not contribute to

16

that assault by making it impossible for clergy couples to thrive in engaging ministries on the one hand, or settling for ministries that ultimately may destroy both their marriage and their ministry, on the other. With the reality that more women are entering into theological education and ministry, compounded with the average age of students entering the ministry slowly growing younger, it is most likely that there will be a continued rise in clergy couples in our denomination. It will become more imperative for churches, presbyteries, and even the denomination to become more proactive and less passive in caring for and supporting clergy couples. Whether pastors are part of a clergy couple or not, the priority in all levels of ministry (parish level to the General Assembly) should be families. We practice this already in different ways: Christian education, pastoral care, and church programs. But pastors (and their families), are often the first exemplars of the church that people notice. We are the leaders that people see in the pulpit on Sunday mornings. As leaders of the church, we come into full view as examples of people of faith as well as parents. Like it or not, we are in the spotlight as examples of faith and family. It doesn't say much when we preach about the importance of families when our own families and relationships are falling apart because we put the priority of being a pastor of a church first. As a church and as a denomination, we need to take this wonderful opportunity to create new models of family-friendly ministries and programs that provide for the discipleship of the new generation.

On the Presbytery level, Committees on Ministry (COM) and Presbytery staffs are the first point of contact for many churches as well as pastors seeking calls. It would be a great asset to everyone if presbytery staffs and COMs took the time, at the very least, to learn about the situations of particular candidates looking into coming to their presbytery. Yes, it takes a great deal of work to place a clergy couple, but perhaps that workload can be lightened if congregations are introduced to and educated about the concept of clergy couples. This benefit would be greatly enhanced if that education and introduction came from an authoritative source such as an Executive Presbyter or chair of the COM, instead of couples themselves.

In talking with countless clergy couples, one tangible idea for the denomination is repeatedly suggested: give congregations a place on Church Information Forms to express their willingness to talk with clergy couples. Furthermore, the "Clergy Couple" question on Personal Information Forms needs to be clarified. In addition to determining that we are a clergy couple, the forms should provide space for us to state that we are a clergy couple looking for calls in the same place or seeking different calls.

Above all, we as a denomination need to provide much prayer and support for every married pastor because in this situation, calls are no longer individual. There are too many lives and a tremendous amount of faith that could be sacrificed if we don't.

Response by Steve Toshio Yamaguchi to Sung and Hope Lee on Marriage

It's All About God's Call

Hope and Sung Lee's story highlights the importance of clarity of call for both pastors and their spouses. The Lees are each unusual in being both a pastor and pastor's spouse at the same time. They advise that such pastors, when seeking a call, give all due consideration to their spouse's call at the same time. This is good advice for every pastor, whether or not the pastor's spouse is a pastor.

Vocation matters. A pastor who moves must be certain that it is God who is calling to that new ministry. A Presbyterian pastor "receives a call"—she or he doesn't just "choose a job." Presbyterians also believe that God calls every believer to a vocation—we don't just "take a job" of our own choosing. Discerning that call is what pastors need to teach and model for all church members, young and old, married and single, when it comes to vocational discernment. In a pastor's home this discernment of call is as important for the pastor's spouse as it is for the pastor—even when the pastor's spouse is not a pastor.

Taking Your Spouse's Call Seriously

Every believer who is married to a pastor is given gifts and a call to mission and ministry every bit as "divine" as their spouse's call. The spouse's call is not second rate. The mutual discernment of calls in the pastor's marriage, as in all Christian marriages, must be made with reciprocal respect for each other's gifting and call to mission. There was an old model in which the male pastor (or businessman) came home one day to announce to his wife that they were moving to a new job in another state—

19

and she was expected to pack up and come along. This model might have seemed to work in the 1950s, but today we witness the tragic fallout of resentment in a pastor's home where this old non-mutual model still gets applied. Marriage is a gift, and one's spouse is a precious gift who is to be treated with all the respect and dignity due one's own flesh. Marriage vows apply to pastors, too. Hope and Sung write: "As a clergy couple we see our call from God as a minister, a spouse, and a parent as exactly that: calls from God." I would ask every pastor and her or his spouse to take the Lee's statement and paraphrase it: "As a *Christian* couple we see our call from God as a *disciple*, spouse, and a parent as exactly that: calls from God" — and then to model that for the church. I am in no way suggesting that a pastor's call to a new ministry is not profoundly important. I am pleading for all married pastors to treat their spouses and their spouse's calls with the same respect.

Taking Your Spouse's Ministry Seriously

Every pastor should want every church member to discover their gifts for ministry and to exercise those gifts in the ministry to which God calls them. A married pastor should wish the same for his or her spouse. Church members can have strong and conflicting expectations of a pastor's spouse; there is no single model for a pastor's spouse today. A pastor's spouse may hear their calling in the life of the congregation as a Sunday School teacher, organist, or choir director. But a pastor's spouse's primary calling to ministry and mission may be as schoolteacher, banker, homemaker, or surgeon. Whatever role they do play in the church where their spouse is the pastor, it should be done because of their gifting and calling for that ministry, not out of pressure from other people's presumptions about the role of a pastor's wife. Sometimes the pastor internalizes the unreasonable expectations of demanding church members, which can lead to undue pressure on the spouse and frustration for the pastor. A married pastor must support their spouse in discerning their particular place in the congregation just as they would support every other member to discern their ministry in the church.

Setting Boundaries: How Not to Exploit Your Spouse

Hope and Sung are wise to remind us that clergy couples need clear boundaries. Their simple question is provocative: "What will you talk about at dinner?" This points to an issue of confidentiality that is good to think about carefully with spouses.

Pastors are invited to share the deepest and most intimate details of people's lives. It is a sacred trust. But a pastor must not presume upon his or her spouse to help bear that burden. Pastors need appropriate places to share the emotional and spiritual burdens of their work. A wise pastor will maintain an informal "council of the wise" who help bear that burden. This "council" could include resources such as a spiritual director, a psychotherapist, or a special covenant group of professional peers. My own "council of the wise" has included a Roman Catholic priest, a doctor of social work, and a Methodist chaplain. Sometimes I pay them and sometimes we're just professional peers. But I keep them available and I use them to help bear the weight of pastoral work.

In my own case, why should my wife provide gratis that for which I pay $100 an hour to a highly trained clinical professional? I am not arguing against sharing concerns for prayer and discernment when it is not gossip and when confidential details are protected. But I want members to know that my wife does not know the details of their sharing. The exception could be if a member specifically requests that I share their details with my wife—I might agree to that if it's appropriate and if my wife is willing. I do not want my wife to bear the stigma of people avoiding her because they are uncomfortable that she might know their embarrassing details. And I do not want people to feel uncomfortable sharing their stories with me because they are afraid that it will leak to my spouse.

Listen Carefully for the Details in the Call

I was pained by Hope's and Sung's disappointment at not receiving compassionate support from their presbytery. It raises an import caveat: listen carefully for the details in the call—before you accept it. The Lees warn: "Don't look to presbyteries to understand your plight." I think that you must look to the presbytery to understand your challenges—but do it before you accept the call. Not all presbyteries are alike and your chemistry will mix with some better than others. But there are many details in a call that must be explored before you receive the call. Size of congregation and salary are popular details, but other factors matter as much or more. What are career opportunities in light of your spouse's vocation? If you are a clergy couple, does the presbytery support/understand/have experience with clergy couples? If your spouse requires special medical attention, does this place have what you need? Does the church have a history of accepting or oppressing pastor's spouses? It is good to trust God, no doubt. But it is also necessary to ask the presbytery and the church to support your spouse and your marriage—and you'd better get the right answer before you accept the call—or maybe it's not the call.

R-E-S-P-E-C-T

Pastors try to treat their members with respect, affirmation, and nurturing support. I think that Hope, Sung, and I are simply entreating married pastors to treat their spouse with that same respect as a starting point—while additionally always remembering the sacrificial nature of our wedding promises.

III

When a Child Comes:
Preparing for Parenthood
But Never Being Ready[1]

Heidi Worthen Gamble

My Story

Before becoming a parent I served two wonderful and challenging calls: the first as co-pastor of a small village church in Alaska with my husband Jason, the second as director and pastor of a homeless ministry in Tacoma, Washington. At the time I thought I knew something of what it meant to follow Christ—to give, to love, to sacrifice. Naturally when I became pregnant with my first child I thought I would be ready for this new calling in my life. I assumed that parenting would be easier than my work as a Minister of Word and Sacrament. But after a long labor, breastfeeding 'round the clock, and hours spent dancing to soothe collicky cries I soon realized that up until the day my oldest daughter was born I had no idea what sacrifice meant. Living on an island in the Bering Sea in Alaska? At least I got to sleep at night! Working on the streets? I went home at the end of the day! Nothing I had done previously compared to the sacrifice of being a mother. Parenting became my new call and it was the toughest one yet.

---

[1] I am especially grateful to Rev. Dr. Elizabeth Nordquist for her support and wise counsel; and to my husband Jason, who took a week's vacation to watch the girls while I wrote.

Shortly after moving to Los Angeles, California, I became pregnant with my oldest daughter Hannah. Previously I had served a call while my husband Jason remained without one, and we agreed that now it was my turn to search for a call. So I spent the first several months applying and interviewing for different positions. As the pregnancy progressed and time went on, however, I changed direction and decided to take some time off. I ended up spending my pregnancy and the first year-and-a-half of parenting as a "minister-at-large and a stay-at-home mom." And I'm so glad I did. I believe I needed that time of retreat to center myself as a mother and to get to know this powerful new little person in my life.

Although I felt grounded in my decision to take time off, truth be told, I had moments of great insecurity about it too. Initially I knew of only one other female colleague who had taken time off to be a parent and I wasn't quite sure of the risks—both to me as a person and to my career as a pastor. Would I be able to get another call with a significant amount of time away from ordained ministry? How would people in churches value my decision to take time off to be a stay-at-home mom? Was I somehow abandoning my ordination vows and my call to ministry? When people asked me what my career was during that time I initially found myself grasping for ways to define my call. While pregnant and guest preaching at churches I nicknamed myself "pregnant pastor on the loose" and during my time off I maintained that I was a Presbyterian pastor who was taking a "leave of absence" from ordained ministry to be a stay-at-home mom.

After almost two years "off" I went back to work as Hunger Action Enabler for the Synod of Southern California and Hawaii. For the first year it was very part-time work, but when Hannah was able to enroll full-time in preschool I not only increased my hours at the Synod, but I also added a second part-time call as Mission Advocate for Pacific Presbytery. Serving two part-time ministries added up to almost full-time work, and my call to ministry and motherhood shifted dramatically. My pace of life was break-neck at times; I received many invitations to preach and lead workshops, speak at meetings, or participate in rallies on the weekends while working during the week. Jason and I had to negotiate our work schedules daily to make it all work, and whenever I could I took Hannah with me, prompting a colleague to nickname me "the Reverend Mother." I often felt like a traveling evangelist to churches, introducing them to a young mother in ministry for the first time. Many churches had to scramble to accommodate childcare needs and I was often met with surprise when I introduced myself as the guest preacher with a young child in-tow. And although I loved the work to which I was called I still felt insecure, only this time my feelings of insecurity centered on my role as mother. Will my daughter be okay? Will she have some kind of permanent psychological damage from so much care outside the home? Does she need more from me than I am able to offer working so much?

Yet now, after the birth of my second daughter Madeleine, I have moved back into a time of retreat from full-time ministry and am mostly at home, serving only very part-time as the Mission Advocate for Pacific Presbytery. Before becoming a parent I imagined typing a sermon in my office while my babies calmly played in a playpen—but what I didn't know is that at precisely the moment one really needs to get something done a baby turns fussy! I imagined taking my babies with me wherever I went—but I didn't think about it depending on whether or not I had babies whose personalities allowed me to do that. I didn't think about how sleep-deprived and physically or emotionally depressed I might feel, how I would need to time outings in-between breast-feedings, how difficult days would be when naps were interrupted and routines broken.

I have likened my rhythm of ministry and parenting in the early years to Jesus' rhythm of time spent engaged with the masses and time spent on retreat. I realize, however, that this is a very different approach to ministry than what has been traditionally done in the past—weaving in and out of calls to ministry in order to parent in the way I feel called. Yet as I meet more young female colleagues from Generation X who choose to have children, I find that I am not alone.

Parenting and Generation X

I am part of a very small, slowly growing population of clergy that is still quite new for the church: women under the age of forty. According to the Manager of the Office of the General Assembly Records, 2.6% of Presbyterian clergy are women under the age of forty in 2006, slightly above 1.6% in 1980.[2] For those of us who decide to have children we engage in a very delicate balancing act between church and family life. And we are making this up as we go! Some of us are negotiating maternity leave policies for the first time in a particular church and negotiating fewer hours, some of us are taking time off and becoming members-at-large, some of us are co-pastoring part-time or finding other part-time ministry positions in governing bodies, and some of us (like myself) are doing a combination of all of the above. What is unique to our generation is that this is not limited to clergy moms; some clergy dads too are negotiating paternity leave policies, choosing to work part-time, and in some instances taking time off to be stay-at-home dads.

What is true for Generation X pastors is a trend for our generation as a whole. According to a survey of 3,020 Generation X parents completed in 2003 by Reach Advisors, a research marketing firm, there are "significant differences between parents from Generation X and their counterparts from the Baby Boom era ... their families take an extreme priority, even more so than the more career-oriented Baby Boomers. Their staunch commitment to family and family time is striking ... .

---

[2] Special thanks to Kris Valerius in the Office of the General Assembly for this information.

26

Instead of trying to fit family into their work life, Generation X parents are more likely to try to fit work into their family life."[3]

The survey also indicates that Generation X moms—although more highly educated than preceding generations—are "more likely than Baby Boomer moms to expect to weave in and out of the workforce over time." Generation X dads, too, are spending more time at home than their Baby Boomer counterparts, but "are more likely to be dissatisfied with the amount of time they spend with their childrearing and household responsibilities"—not because they think it's too much but because Generation X dads want to spend even more time on the homefront.[4] This generational trend is what some are calling a "neo-traditionalist" approach to parenting—having a career and then choosing to pare down or step down from it for a time to raise children.

What is it that Generation X parents are seeking today? When I talk with moms from my generation there are common themes: we don't want somebody else to raise our children; we want to be there for our children's "firsts" and experience them growing up; we want to do a good job of parenting. We're also looking for a healthy balance between work and family life. Charlotte Fishman, an employment attorney and executive director of *Pick Up the Pace*, a nonprofit organization dedicated to women's advancement in the workplace writes: "Increasingly, both men and women seek a world in which the spurious community of overwork yields to a genuine community supporting the common welfare." [5] More importantly, she indicates that the priority of work-family balance is not only a shift happening in the upper classes for those who are privileged to have options to stay at home or work part-time, but rather a

---

[3] Executive summary of study conducted by: Reach Advisors, *Generation X Parents: From Grunge to Grown Up* (June 2004), p. 1. Used by permission.
[4] Ibid., 2.
[5] Charlotte Fishman, "Mothers At Work are Canaries in the Mine" *WomensENews: www.womensenews.com* (October 19, 2005): 2.

seismic shift in thinking that extends to the full-time workforce as well, including the working classes as well. In fact she goes so far as to call this "a major, dislocating social transformation" of the current generation.[6]

This is good news, because parenting has become an almost daunting task today. Although parenting has never been an easy job there are some peculiarities to our postmodern context that I would argue make the job of raising children with positive self-esteem and strong core values more difficult than in times past: a product-driven, "hyper-sexualized,"[7] self-absorbed popular culture that audaciously targets children and continues to find new ways of gaining access to their time and attention; an increasingly isolationist culture that understands parenting as an individual pursuit and does not raise children communally; and a multiplicity of authoritative voices and "information overload" on parenting that creates moral and spiritual confusion and cuts off access to our own intuition. Add to that the realities of things like a public school system in serious jeopardy, a highly competitive global economy, a frenzy-paced lifestyle, and an increasingly anxious and fearful world since 9/11, and we've got a challenging context for raising children.

A Holistic Understanding of Call

What I find I must do to navigate through the waters of work and parenting is to engage in intentional, prayerful discernment. When the balance is right my work gives me joy and energy that spills over into wonderful quality time with my children and the delight of being with my children brings insight, maturity and efficiency to my work. But finding the right balance takes wisdom, and learning to develop a keen sense of discernment is quiet, humble, inner spiritual work. I

---

[6] Ibid, 3.

[7] Danny and Polly Duncan Collum, "Parenting Under Siege" *Sojourners Magazine* (January 2006): 1.

find I must learn to let go of many things, such as my expectations of success, my own ego's many hidden agendas, and a clean house. For me it takes prayer, journaling, a wise spiritual director, and the support of my community: my family, colleagues, church family, and good friends.

It also takes asking new questions. Instead of asking more traditional discernment questions such as: Where is God calling me? I find it more helpful to ask: To what is God calling me today, at this time, in this season of my life? My spiritual director often asks me: "What time is it?" I find it helpful when I can remember to ask myself that question. Is it time to sleep or eat? Preach a sermon or rock my baby? Take my preschooler to a rally for justice or stay home and nurse her cold? And I am reminded to trust that the God who has called me both to motherhood in the home and to ministry in the world will not forsake or abandon me but will make a way where there is no way—time where there is no time.

Deep within the Reformed tradition is the religious vocation of all of life's work, including domestic toil. One of the significant shifts of the Reformation was that the home became the monastery, as Bonnie Miller-McLemore writes in her book *Also A Mother: Work and Family as Theological Dilemma.*[8] But she also points out that ironically, the PC(U.S.A.) and other mainline Protestant traditions have been especially quiet about what she defines as "generative responsibilities," or responsibilities at home and at work. "Men and women, most seem to agree, are equal before God. But exactly what this means for the common life of work and love in churches, in families, and in jobs is less clear."[9] Our current cultural practice is to make this a private issue endlessly negotiated between married partners in the home but I would argue this is also about community, about a holistic understanding of vocation in the reconstituted family of Jesus

---

[8] Bonnie J. Miller-McLemore, *Also A Mother: Work and Family as Theological Dilemma* (Nashville, TN: Abingdon Press, 1994), p. 36.
[9] Ibid., 37.

Christ. It is not just about finding the right balance for me in my individual marital relationship and family life, it is also about living into a vision of the kingdom community where all are loved, cherished and made whole.

Thinking The Faith: A Time of New Forms, New Cloaks

"No one sews a piece of unshrunk cloth on an old cloak; otherwise, the patch pulls away from it, the new from the old, and a worse tear is made." (Mark 2:21) In the passages preceding this verse Jesus is being criticized for eating with sinners and outcasts and allowing his disciples to eat instead of fast. But with Jesus, in his preaching and manifestation of the kingdom of God, something new has come and it calls for new forms to hold it. The traditional forms of fasting and maintaining purity codes are no longer appropriate to what Jesus' ministry is about. So, too, with the current forms and structures of the workplace today, including the church's traditional expectations of the pastoral office. We know the consequences of working too much. Succumbing to too many demands is dangerous and tears at our souls: it leads to burnout, stress, illness—all of which are toxic to our children and to us. It is a time of new "cloaks," new rhythms, new and more holistic ways of understanding work, call and family life.

How can we begin to live more deeply into our calling as Christ's kingdom community and intentionally love and support those who are caring for children, including our clergy families? Can we imagine some kind of national family leave policy with a grant program for pastors of struggling churches? A "family care" representative from a presbytery's Committee on Ministry who ministers to clergy families with young children? A designated deacon in churches to care for families with young children?

Can we imagine a community where women and men can work and love in a way that provides for them *and* allows for space and time to care for their children, or aging parents, or siblings with a disability, or all who are in more vulnerable stages of life? What would it look like? How might the church be on the cutting edge of this? Can we invite people into an alternative community that models the kingdom values of love, service, justice and peace for our children and for all of us? Let us pray that it may be so.

Response by Steve Toshio Yamaguchi
to Heidi Worthen Gamble on Parenting

Heidi's story warms my heart and gives me great hope for the Church, for Hannah and Madeleine, for Heidi and Jason themselves, and for other young clergy parents who take inspiration from Heidi's witness. How good to hear a story well told by a thoughtful, self-aware, intentionally Christian Gen X pastor. Previous generations raised children in a world of different expectations, possibilities, perils, and cultural supports. In a changed and more challenging world, Heidi offers hope for a new model of pastor parent.

You Get One Shot

Heidi recognizes that being a parent opens up a new world of learning about giving and love and sacrifice—and I would add vulnerability. It is a world that continues to expand in unimaginable ways. Pastoral ministry also affords continually new depths of learning and intimacy beyond what we imagined. A pastor gets to walk and sit with people in their deepest longings and fears up to the brink of death and beyond. A pastor gets to walk through that portal with people, sharing the hope of the resurrection where lives have been shattered. A pastor gets to witness the miraculous growth of faith and healing in those who are bearing impossible burdens. It's cosmically important stuff. It's intimate, seductive stuff. Parenting also affords these new depths of learning and intimacy, and as Heidi has learned, even more profoundly. One key difference: in parenting you get one shot per child. They grow up faster than you could have ever imagined.

When a pastor becomes a parent, the pastoral needs and opportunities in the congregation don't go away. They are still as demanding and seductive. These people also pay your salary. When they are happy with you their positive strokes can make you feel better; when they are disappointed with you their complaints hurt. In the face of all that pressure, I still plead the case that there is nothing worth sacrificing your parenting vocation for. I would sum up the whole point of this little chapter in this one line: the church can always call another pastor, but only you can be the parent to your child.

Pastors will always have more opportunities for profound spiritual encounters with members. It's the cyclical nature of pastoral work and life itself. This is not to minimize the profundity of it all, but if you botch a pastoral interaction (and you will, more than once), there will be another opportunity to botch it again. There will be other congregants to care for. For most pastors there will even be other congregations to care for. And if the congregation grows it means more people with more needs and more complex programs and more organization that needs more attention. More study, more prayer, more planning, more leaders to manage, maybe even more staff to supervise—there can always be more.

As a parent you get one opportunity to give it your best shot. It's a time-limited opportunity. Heidi is taking advantage of this opportunity in a way that she'll always cherish and never regret. When my daughters were small I tried hard to dedicate time to them as a priority over more evening meetings and more work to do. I tried to be intentional about resisting the incessant seduction of more church work in a constantly growing and changing congregation. I could have done better in many ways. But one thing I did was to sing to the girls at bedtime.

I use my guitar to emote and communicate my heart. When our older daughter was a baby, I started playing for her very quietly at bedtime. It helped her fall to sleep. I added singing. It became nightly. It continued when our second daughter was born. Together we developed a repertoire of bedtime songs: some silly songs, some hymns, some scripture and prayers put to tunes, some songs I wrote for them, and some funny songs we wrote together. It was the nightly bedtime ritual and they would fall asleep while I played and sang for them. At one point they were so habituated to daddy's songs that when I traveled I had to leave them a recording of me singing good night songs. It worked.

Some "specialists" write that children should be allowed to "put themselves to sleep," even if it means crying themselves to sleep. These folks say that it is a disservice to children to let them become dependent on anything (singing, back rubs, hand holding, sitting nearby) for going to sleep. I wasn't buying it. This was a gift that I could share with them and it gave us a unique connection and bonding worth more than gold. I invested more than a decade singing songs to my girls every night. I think it's one of the best things I did as a dad. (And now, my children can crash at night just fine on their own, without daddy singing, thank you very much.)

The parent-pastor must seize the day for it will not cycle around again, unlike an Advent program or a fall stewardship campaign or a summer children's ministry. No matter how desperately I might wish to, I could not go back and make up that song-singing time after they had grown. I had to do it back in the day. There is no *ex post facto* clause. *Carpe diem.*

"You're Weird, Dad"

I think Gen X parents are better suited for this than builders or boomers were. Christian parents (pastors or otherwise) need to raise counter-cultural kids in this postmodern, post-Christian world. This requires a whole different worldview of parenting. There was a very different time in a previous generation (or two) when a pastor could hope that their kids would keep their noses clean and not grate

34

against or stick out too much from the culture at large. "Be good kids. Fit in with everybody else. Don't make waves." Today the last thing in the world I want is for my kids to fit into the culture at large. I want my children to learn how to make waves for God's justice. I do not want my children to fit into a world of greed and materialism, injustice and violence, where human dividing walls cultivate fear and hatred of those who are different. My wife and I hope that our home is cultivating an alternative community where the values of the Kingdom of God are lived. We try to model (not just speak) to our children about being counter-cultural, about integrity and honesty and justice and grace. In our house "you're weird" is a high compliment; to be called "normal" is a bit of a slight.

It takes time to build community. It takes time to build a home. It takes time to invest in your children so that they believe that you believe in them. It takes time to lead and coach them to do unpopular things, to cultivate in them the courage and confidence to do things that nobody else is doing. It takes discipline to put school performances and time to play and explore with children and good vacations on your calendar and then to refuse to let any other meeting or work crowd them out. And the time for young parents to do that is now and this opportunity won't come around again.

If you are thinking, "Oh Heidi, parenting is always parenting, kids are always the same, and it's not any different for you today than when we raised our kids" – I think that you're wrong and Heidi is right. It's a qualitatively different world today that Gen X parents and their children face. If you're of a previous generation and you can't see Heidi's point, please listen more carefully to young parents. Please be open to recalibrating your standards.

Heidi is absolutely right that parenting as a pastor is a matter of spiritual discernment. It's not about career planning and time management. It's about owning the complexity of our multiple vocations and recognizing that our vocation to be a parent is more intense and more time-limited than our vocation to be a pastor. It's about being attentive enough to discern the voice of God calling us to our particular vocations, one day at a time. Seize the day!

IV

The Essence of the Pastoral Call –
Success is not Faithfulness:
Living and Interpreting the Difference

William "Bill" A.C. Golderer

I love movies. Most of the time I watch a movie in order to escape the worldly pressures and expectations and cares to be found every time I power up my PDA or check my voice mail. I like almost every genre of film—comedies, drama, noir— whatever. One criterion that must be in place for me to truly enjoy the film is that it needs to transport me into another world. This world needn't be fantasy. It can be a hard and grueling world, filled with harsh realities and truths, so long as it provides me with an escape from my own preoccupations and concerns—however trivial they may be.

With that said, every so often I see a film—or a scene from one—that depicts so vividly something I am struggling with or speaks so pointedly to my situation that I cannot get it out of my mind.

One scene that struck me in this fashion is relevant to the topic of this chapter. The film is called *Scent of a Woman*, starring Al Pacino, who brilliantly plays a disgraced and disillusioned Colonel Frank Slade. Col. Slade forges an unlikely mentoring relationship with Charlie Simms (Chris O'Donnell) after the colonel's family off-loads his care to the young prep-schooler over Thanksgiving weekend. Pacino's character is an alcoholic and blind and he takes this prep school boy under his wing to teach him a thing or two about romance, the city of New York, and most of all what it means to possess integrity. The movie is full of great lines, but the scene that hit me between the eyes occurs when the colonel—who is fumbling around drunk and depressed trying to make his way through a labyrinth of household obstacles—calls out in desperation to no one in particular, a memorable line that I have since made into a guttural prayer of petition.

"Can I get a little help please? I am in the dark here!"

Behind these simple lines of dialogue lies a profound desperation about the limitations Pacino's character is experiencing because of his inability to see where he is going. He is frustrated since he knows there is a way to successfully navigate through the impediments in his way to the destination he has in mind. His anguish and pain stem from the realization that he will need help from someone with better vision of the path in order for him to get there. He knows there is a path even though he can't see it. There are impediments in his way. He is crying out for help—for a better set of eyes—to guide him in the direction he needs to go.

God is funny like that. I have had the experience more than once of sitting on a hard chair and poring over a scripture passage for some time looking for a word of clarity or a hint that this whole enterprise of pastoral ministry isn't some kind of cruel joke. Frustrated, I pop in a DVD or listen to some music or lift some weights, and I get a telegram from the Holy Other—or at least that's how it feels to me sometimes.

The film is good—no doubt—but the dialogue spoke powerfully to me in large part due to the vocational circumstances (or crisis) I found myself in at the time. It was just two years ago when I left behind any official job or call within the church. I struggled mightily with this job from the day I walked into the office. Being there every day was a chore. I was disillusioned by the goals and objectives we were shooting for organizationally and I felt powerless to do anything about it. This was all bad enough but the fact that I was doing this under the auspices of the practice of Christian ministry made it all the more painful. I felt like I had sacrificed a lot to pursue pastoral ministry and I was willing to sacrifice a lot, but I thought I would get a greater sense of satisfaction from trying to pursue a sense of call.

After what we call in church-newsletter speak, "a prolonged time of discernment" and what I now refer to as "a prolonged time of frustration mixed in with a fair dose of disillusionment about what the ministry was all about"—it was clear that it was time to move on.

Leaving was painful and it left me reeling, not only about my new status as "unemployed" (unemployable?). It led at the same time to an even more difficult period of time when I felt I needed to pick up this object called ministry and look at it from every side and decide whether I should keep it or junk it—like an old popcorn maker. After enrolling in a refresher bartending course and lamenting whether I had been wasting my time all along with the preparation for and practice of ministry, I found myself praying over and over again the prayer lifted from a Hollywood screenplay:

"Can I get a little help please? I am in the dark here!!"

This was a difficult time filled with a lot of grueling physical exercise and even more grueling prayer work. What emerged from this time two years later was a deep conviction about two things I know as surely as I know my name. I came up for air confident that:

- The practice of faithful pastoral ministry in the context of community is viable and necessary not only for perpetuating the church as an institution, but also for the transformation of society.

39

- The pursuit of faithful pastoral ministry can be frustrated, waylaid and even thwarted more than we would like to admit by impediments that are in the path.

One hard truth is this: just because one is ordained as a Minister of the Word and Sacrament (as we refer to it in my tradition) and serving a congregation doesn't necessarily mean one is involved in a practice of ministry. And another hard truth is that just because there is a sign outside a building that proclaims to the neighborhood and the world—we are a church!—doesn't mean as a point of unassailable fact that what is going on inside has anything to do with a community of people who are looking to follow, however falteringly, the life and example of Jesus Christ.

Now if you think—after a grand total of 36 years of taking up space here on earth and approaching a mere decade of ordained pastoral ministry—I am claiming to have all the answers, I don't. But after a considered (as opposed to considerable) time spent in the practice of what I thought was faithful ministry and after a painful time spent in exile away from and disillusioned with its practice and now after a wary but passionate return to the enterprise, I can claim only what I believe to be the essence of pastoral ministry. Perhaps it will strike a chord.

My sincere belief is that more than ever before for this crucial time in the life of the church the essence of pastoral ministry involves testing the spirits, motivations and desires of the pastor as well as of the community to discern those things that are on the path to faithful ministry and what represents an obstacle to its pursuit.

Let's go backwards, since that's how I do almost everything. Going back for a moment to Al Pacino's character, the colonel in "Scent of a Woman," the thing that was giving him pain (psychical as well as physical) was his knowledge of the obstacles that stood between him and the path he was

40

pursuing. He knew they were there. He knew that bumping up against them would be harmful. He was frustrated that he couldn't see them so that he might avoid them.

"Can I get a little help please? I am in the dark here!!"

Unlike Pacino's character, I have experienced the obstacles and impediments to the faithful practice of ministry as things that are in plain view but are too infrequently seen or understood for what they are. The punch line for this chapter—the essence of pastoral ministry—is the capacity to see these impediments more clearly with one's heart—first for oneself and then alongside others in the community. I believe this capacity for "heart-sight" is what lies at the core of what ministers need most to practice for themselves and along with others in the communities in which they are called to serve. The size and shape and form of these spiritual impediments are specific to each ministry context, but I have yet to visit one where formidable obstacles have not been stubbornly and seductively in place. The craft of the minister in community is to learn to see them for what they are, to be brave enough to name them as such, and to find the resources within and beyond the community to discover how best to go around, over, or through them on the path toward the faithful practice of ministry.

How about an example of a spiritual impediment from everyday conversation?

I was recently at a party with a number of people I don't know. See if you recognize the flow of the following excerpt from a conversation I had there.

> Man in nice suit: Hey, I don't think we've met. I'm Dan.
> Bill: Nice to meet you Dan, I'm Bill.
> Dan: So Bill, what do you do?

If I were a courtroom attorney like Sam Waterson on *Law and Order* I would stand up and say, "Objection!" each time a conversation took this turn so early. I decided shouting "objection" would appear weird at such a party, but inside I want to jump out of my skin any time I am asked that question right off the bat. The question is innocent enough on the surface. But I have come to believe it is unlikely I am going to learn anything I most want or need to know about this person by asking this question. And no one is going to know what I think I want them to know about me either.

It is not only for this reason I find the question objectionable. The question triggers an internal red flag signaling that I am about to bump up against a spiritual impediment that I have long battled. "What do I do?" you ask? I pray. I write. I try to give some comfort to people awaiting test results. I look for signs of the realm of God breaking into this heartbreaking world. That's not the answer that is expected, welcomed or will likely be given in this informal exchange.

On one level, the question shouldn't be so objectionable… it's just a question right? But my fear in answering it in the traditional way, "I am an ordained Presbyterian minister," is that if I reduce my answer to the lowest common denominator—I know what is likely to happen. The answer will be given, an assessment will be made, an assessment based on the often mercenary nature of the ways in which we evaluate and are evaluated by others. The answer will be plotted somewhere on what I call the Cultural Success Index.

The Cultural Success Index is an apparatus of my own invention that defines, characterizes and ultimately functions to "plot" people (and a myriad of other things) somewhere on a continuum of what a market economy deems valuable. It can apply to everything from career, to hobbies, interests, even charities.

Cultural Success Index

Now we all know that Dan was just being friendly but I am sensitive to this because I see within this question a piece of a difficult spiritual impediment that confronts those attempting to practice faithful ministry. I know more than a few ministers of my generation who are ambivalent about being ministers. And no wonder! The church has done and continues to do some wretched things as a part of its witness. But apart from that or perhaps at an even deeper level than that, I know many ministers who have shared with me that they feel "worth-less" in the eyes of culture. Some have shared that this has not only to do with what they earn (which certainly doesn't help) but also with something that is more difficult to articulate. Aside from finding oneself neck-deep in a profession about which the culture is more than a little ambivalent, in institutions that seem to be sputtering at best—if they aren't in outright freefall—many young pastors have shared with me a gnawing sense that the practice of ministry falls somehow far outside the aspirations of our culture and the values it blesses, even—and especially—if they are doing it faithfully.

This is at the core of the spiritual challenges I face at the personal level in the practice of faithful ministry in my context. I have seen, as if for the first time, all the ways in which my practice of Christian ministry previously was informed by a desire to secure for myself a respectable position on the Cultural Success Index. Prior to becoming ordained, I always wanted my peers and friends and people who first met me to be impressed. Who doesn't want that? But after my ordination, I wanted—often unknowingly—to pass muster on the Cultural Success Index just in my "chosen field," which happened to be ministry.

Following my time of disillusionment and exile and now on the hard road back to my current practice of ministry in community, I understand the folly of trying to pursue both faithful ministry on the one hand, and attempting with equal energy to secure an enviable position on the Cultural Success Index.

Ministers are immersed in a culture with appetites for things that never appeared on the radar screen of Jesus' priorities. Before persons can practice pastoral ministry, they need first to see with their heart the spiritual impediments that stand between them as individuals and what the gospel commends as the way to follow Christ. For me, the first step was to recognize and overcome (to the best of my capacity) the yearning that resided within me to register a respectable position on the Cultural Success Index.

For someone whom Christ has called to service, becoming aware of vexing spiritual impediments is hard work. The impediments that one encounters on one's path are legion and are likely different from mine. Whatever they are, acknowledgment that they exist and commitment of energy to transcend them is an endangered discipline. It requires effort to navigate around these impediments. Self-awareness in relation to these obstacles is only one component of what I understand to be essential to the practice of faithful ministry.

Earning A Seat on the CSI or the FFI?

The minister who recognizes the spiritual impediments within herself must also be committed to doing so alongside and on behalf of the community she finds herself in. The minister is called upon to do so many things—too many things in fact—week after week. And yet, I am convinced that the body of Christ's witness going into the institutional church's uncertain future will be exponentially more powerful and more faithful if a greater number of my colleagues would spend more energy discerning the spiritual impediments that stand in the way of the community's ability to provide a witness in their particular context.

The great blessing of my current context—Broad Street Ministry—is that there are an extraordinary number of people who are willing to engage in what I have come to refer to as "first order thinking" about the impediments that most directly threaten our work and witness. It is a new faith community that is committed to mining the stories of scripture and the Christian tradition for guidance about how to live faithfully in Christian community and to work together to watch for and participate in God's work of bringing in the New Realm.

These are good aims. But much of our work circles back around to seeing and acknowledging spiritual impediments in the path. We have identified a few of them, with God's help, and this has enabled us to carve out an ethos that seeks to steer a course around, over and sometimes through them. One such impediment that the community recognizes can be uncovered by returning to the conversation I earlier began with Dan—remember, from the party?

> Dan: I see ... A minister, that's nice. (spoken as you
> see Dan struggling to gather something else
> to say). Where is your church—how many
> members do you have?
> Bill (about to cry): Well ...

The impediment our community has recognized is that the success obsession that dominates our culture has also seeped into every element of our living—including the life and work of the church. Rather than seeing the Cultural Success Index as a threat to its witness, the church too often is seduced by it or at least nestles up to it. It measures its impact with the same tools as our market economy—sometimes without realizing the devastating spiritual consequences of doing so.

Rather than prophetically redefining the cultural appetite for expansion, increase, consumption, numerical growth and more of everything, church communities stand inside these criteria of success and measure themselves against them. They have created for themselves their own Congregational Success Index that apes the culture's obsession with things that trend upward (and I don't mean toward heaven). The way I as a representative and leader of the faith community answer Dan's question about our community's size—which on the surface is simple enough—can tell you a lot about how much our community has internalized the values of a culture that equates more with better. For us, our practice of community witness begins with the giving of intentional answers to questions like these and learning to recognize the impediments to faithful ministry that lie in the shadows behind them.

Congregations looking to work with ministers of the Word and Sacrament on this defining spiritual practice will be willing to engage the first-order questions and underlying expectations that align so closely with the consumer culture. Prayer and truth-telling may well uncover a pastor's, unreasonable and, I dare say, unfaithful expectations.

Preoccupation with membership roles may be replaced with a passionate pursuit of understanding about why certain demographics are missing from the communion's gathering. This is more than a semantic difference. Pastoral search committees may begin to look for more than excellent managers who can efficiently implement (and grow) existing programming and instead search for leaders who can help raise questions about whether the community is pursuing the correct path in its life and work. Imagination would trump implementation. Depth would trounce growth. Disciplined discernment would be valued over efficiency and "effectiveness."¹

Our community believes that the Christian community you commit to cannot be understood by the numbers on the membership rolls, attendance at its programs, the size (largesse?) of its budget and endowment. Whether the congregation that has 5,000 members or 5 cannot give Dan or anyone else immersed in the Cultural Success Index reliable data about the relative health, faithfulness, daring, imagination, compassion or anything else that goes into the work of discipleship.

Broad Street has taught me over and over again not to hunger and thirst for a prominent seat on the Congregational Success Index—a wholly owned subsidiary of the Cultural Success Index—and an impediment in our path. We struggle with it constantly. We are intentionally working to identify the obstacles that stand between us and making our way onto the Disciple Faithfulness Index. Its criteria are not yet formulated except, to say, "we know it when we see it."

From my vantage point, the essence of pastoral ministry for the next era of Christian witness will encourage pastoral leadership with intentional, candid, and courageous work to cultivate hearts that can see the impediments to faithful Christian witness as well as confidence in God's power to lead us past these impediments in order to continue on the path God lays before us.

Response by John T. Galloway, Jr.
to Bill Golderer on The Essence of the Call

Not only do I have enormous respect for Bill Golderer's ministry and cherish our friendship, it seems, in addition, that we have similar tastes in movies. I, too, loved *Scent of a Woman*, though I opt for the tango scene as my favorite. But I must admit that Al Pacino's line "Can I get a little help please? I am in the dark here!" is a line that will preach. Haven't we all felt that? Thank you, Bill, for holding it up for us as an articulation of our commonly felt plight.

And thank you, too, for giving language to our not so subtle craving for high scores on the Cultural Success Index. We want too much for the Dans of this world to think well of us. We like to dazzle on the social scene and impress former school chums, new friends and all our in-laws. It feels good to have "successful" numbers on mammon's scorecard.

Bill is right. The Cultural Success Index is for many a pastor an impediment that trips up too many of us.

By way of response, I just want to make sure that we all understand a very basic fact. Wanting cultural success is not the real culprit here. Indexes are. Whenever we set any measuring device alongside our ministry we tend to push and pull and bend our ministry to measure up. Cultural success is only one way to calibrate the index.

I would suggest that cultural failure might just as easily be a way to succeed on someone else's gauge. Over coffee at a denominational gathering, Pat might ask me, "How many members do you have?" and I cringe because I know that on Pat's index having a large number of white suburbanites marks me for being a shallow huckster, marketing pious pablum. To win points with Pat I should have a small, culturally mixed group in a more "relevant" sounding locale: like an urban store front, or among the rural poor. While more of us lose our way by following an upwardly mobile path, we can just as easily drift from our calling by intentionally opting for downward mobility. Indexes can be deceptive as well as seductive.

We need to remind ourselves that, when in John 15 Jesus talked to his disciples about bearing fruit, he was very careful never to spell out exactly what he meant by fruit. As Bill is suggesting, too many of us impose our own definition on what the word "fruit" means to our ministry and we do so at our own peril. The Rev. Ms. Alice believes that to be fruitful means that her congregation will have lots of members and an even higher worship attendance. Alas, once she thinks she knows what "fruitful" means, she will unwittingly develop an idolatrous addiction to whatever ups the numbers on her "fruitful ministry index."

The Rev. Mr. Tom goes after big giving as his way of feeling fruitful. For Charlotte the goal is how many members go on her mission trips. For Charlie the sign of a fruitful ministry is how many converts he gets, as if he were the one who "got" them.

Now, let's be honest. There is something insidiously therapeutic about tangible markers in our ministry. I will go so far as to suggest that we need to nurse our "tangible index need" from time to time to keep our sanity, as long as we are aware of what we are doing and don't take it too seriously. For example, I have often told people about one of the greatest days in my ministry. In my seminary days, campus scuttlebutt had it that no self-respecting pastor would ever run the mimeo machine. (I have discovered recently that telling this to younger pastors is met with a blank stare. So for young readers I point out that this old duffer is referring to the mimeo machine which existed before Xerox. It was a manually cranked, inky way to run off copies of the bulletin and other papers.) Anyway, one afternoon back around 1970 in upstate New York the secretary had to be out of the office, so it fell to me to run one hundred copies of some five page thingamabob. I did it. I cranked the wheel and out the copies came. Then I realized I loved it. I went home so energized that I took my wife downtown for an expensive dinner. Whereas most days I'd come home having no idea whether I had done anything of any value for the kingdom, that afternoon I knew I had done some good. A stack of yellow paper to my left had been blank. But because I had cranked the crank repetitiously a stack of yellow paper piled up to my right with stuff, the same stuff, on each sheet. I did that. I tell you I strutted across the street late that afternoon. I bounded into the manse. "Honey, your man is the man. Let me tell you what this dude made happen with my own little hands." Seminaries should have been advising us to run the mimeo as often as we could.

Tangible ministry markers can be therapeutic. We need a few from time to time. Just remember that when tangible markers become an index to define our ministry, watch out. It is time for prayerful re-evaluation of our call.

Could it be that our real problem in ministry is an unwillingness to live with ambiguity? Could it be that when a pastor cries out "Can I get a little help please? I am in the dark here," our frustration is not that we know there is a way for us that we are too blind to see. Our frustration, indeed our terrifying realization is that those who see most clearly can tell us there are precious few if any "right ways." In fact being sure you have found THE way may be the source of the problem for most troubled ministries. Perhaps faithful ministry requires us to admit that we are not supposed to find the right way to do what we do. Could it be that stumbling, bruising our shins, falling flat on our faces is just something that inevitably happens in this ambiguous calling we have chosen to accept?

I have always resonated with the narrative in Joshua 3. "When you see the ark of the covenant of the Lord your God being carried by the levitical priests, then you shall set out from your place. Follow it, so that you may know the way you should go, for you have not passed this way before." (vs. 2b-4a) Whether because we are in a post-Constantinian or post-modern world, or perhaps owing to the trauma of 9/11, one thing is increasingly clear to us as we stand in the early years of the twenty-first century: we have not passed this way before. We are ministering more than ever in uncharted territory. Our ambiguity is even more ambiguous.

I conclude by bringing us back to the movie theatre. There was another film title that may help those of us who, like Al Pacino, are "in the dark here." Joshua was told to follow the ark. Good advice. I'd love to follow the ark. But Harrison Ford captured our time in a movie that was not titled "Raiders of the Ark that is Just Ahead." No. The movie in which he starred was "Raiders of the Lost Ark." God has called us to minister in a world where the ark is lost and we don't even know for sure if it exists at all anymore. Not only have we never been this way before. But we can't find an ark to guide us.

Doing ministry requires a radical trust because the fruit we are to bear is undefined, the ark is lost and any index we employ can become an idolatrous diversion and barrier to faithful service.

Response by Thomas W. Gillespie
to Bill Golderer on The Essence of the Call

Pastor Golderer and I have practiced ordained Christian ministry in different places and, especially, at different times. Our experiences of ministry are not at all the same, and yet I can resonate to his concern about the "spiritual impediments" that are the constant companions of all ministers in our American culture. The "Cultural Success Index" (CSI) may be his terminology, but the temptation to measure success and failure in ministry by its criteria, and thus establish one's sense of self-worth has been around for at least as long as I have been ordained. What puzzles me about his essay, however, is what this has to do with "the essence of pastoral call."

Presbyterians, as well as other communions, have long believed that God calls people into the ordained ministry of the Church. John Calvin distinguished two basic ways in which this occurs. One he called "the secret call" which people hear in a variety of ways and under different circumstances. The other he termed "the public call" in which God speaks through the Church to those recognized as having recognizable gifts for ministry. Of the two, Calvin thought the latter more important than the former. Yet as the tradition has developed over time we Presbyterians have come to rely upon a combination of the two ways, relying heavily upon the public voice of the Church to test and possibly confirm the secret call heard by potential candidates.

I heard the call of God to ministry quite unexpectedly as an eighteen-year-old Marine. But it was tested and confirmed by the elders of my local church and then by the presbytery, which put me through the academic, theological, and psychological hoops until, upon graduation from seminary, I was ready to receive a call from a congregation. That was the final test in the process, at least initially. I was ordained only when that call came and was approved by my presbytery. What I sense Bill Golderer struggling with is the question concerning what confirms life in ministry *after* one is ordained and installed in a particular ministry. Is it the ecclesial version of the "Cultural Success Index"? My answer to that question is an unqualified No, on the one hand, and a highly qualified Maybe on the other. For by the standards of the CSI I have known both success and failure in ministry, but without ever doubting my call. Let me share my story.

Ministry for me began in 1954 as the organizing pastor of a new church development in Garden Grove, California (Yes, I know Robert Schuller). Young ministers today cannot even imagine how different the world was in those years. Our town grew from 3,500 residents in 1950 to 117,000 a decade later. The orange orchards were uprooted in favor of ever-new housing, predominantly for young marrieds. The average age in our community was twenty-five, with 47% of the population under nineteen years of age. Garden Grove was full of World War II veterans working their first jobs, buying their first homes, and having their first children. And they poured into the churches. I recall one new member class when ninety people showed up, most of whom I had never called on. We were organized by the old Los Angeles Presbytery with 161 charter members and received over 1,800 people into the congregation during the twelve years of our pastorate there. Together we transformed a vacant five-acre lot into a beautiful campus, complete with sanctuary, church school facilities, fellowship hall, office suite — the whole nine yards. That was pretty heady stuff according to the "Congregational Success Index." And there is no doubt that it had a profound impact upon my young life and self-understanding. But I can also say that it was done with as much honesty, transparency, and integrity as I could muster. My people encouraged me to preach the gospel of Jesus Christ as clearly and winsomely as I knew how to do, and they supported me in doing it. Did I make mistakes? More than I care to admit. Yet the congregation forgave my youthful foolish errors when necessary and gave me freedom to grow through it all.

My second call, however, was a different story. Looking back upon the year 1966, I still find it difficult to believe that I willingly moved to the San Francisco Bay Area in the midst of the social unrest that characterized the Sixties. The Haight-Ashbury was but eighteen miles up El Camino Real from our church in the village of Burlingame, representing as it did the home of the Hippies and their cultural revolution. The University of California across the Bay was on fire with the Free Speech Movement and Viet Nam War protests. The Black Panthers were flexing their muscles in Oakland, and the Symbionese Liberation Army was robbing banks and kidnapping Patty Hearst. It was a different world from Garden Grove, a different church, and a different ministry.

Some felt that my distinguished predecessor had been eased out because of his strong stand on a fair housing referendum in California and resented me for succeeding him, while others were certain that anyone coming out of Orange County had to be a member of the John Birch Society. Put simply, I went from a congregation that was united to one that was polarized, from a church where I could seemingly do no wrong to one where it felt like I could do no right. Add to this the fact that of our alleged 2,100 members fully one-third no longer lived in San Mateo County, much less Burlingame and its immediate environs. So in my first two years we cleaned our roles to 1,400, and much of that represented a soft membership. I was not doing well by the standards of the "Church Success Index." And did it affect me? Yes, indeed. I felt that I was failing in ministry without even trying.

The crucial issue for me, however, was not the size of the membership but the resistance among some to my preaching ministry. There were folks leaving the church because, as they put it, "there was too much Jesus coming from the pulpit." I am flexible enough to compromise on many things, but Jesus is not one of them. Who he is and the redemptive significance of what he did is for me the heart of the gospel, and it was precisely to the proclamation of the gospel that I was called. It was a painful time for me and the family, and I even considered accepting one of two different calls to promising churches that came to me during the summer of my second year there. In fact I shared this with my presbytery executive, who said to me, "Tom, I know it has been a tough two years, and if you decide to leave I will support you. But I must tell you that I hope you will stay. What you are trying to do needs to be done, and there is no assurance that it will be if you resign." The drive home that day, across the San Mateo Bridge and causeway, provided an opportunity to have it out with the Lord God Almighty. And about half-way across that sixteen mile span it suddenly occurred to me that in all my years I had never been asked by God to do anything that was painful for the sake of Christ. That settled it, and I walked into the kitchen that evening and announced to my long-suffering wife that we were staying where we had been planted. She could believe it.

Well, we did stay—for seventeen years—and may well have retired from that church had the call to Princeton Seminary not come to us. It was a different congregation when we finally did depart from the one we had originally known. I leave it to the Lord to determine whether or not that difference was a positive or negative one. But it was then and is today a healthy church with deep involvement in its community and outreach to the world. My point is that, for me at least, integrity in ministry comes from faithfulness to the gospel as best any of us understands it. In my experience, that sometimes leads to remarkable numerical growth and, while at other times in a different place it entails a shrinking membership. The important thing in either situation is what God is doing in the lives of people through the gospel of Christ and the power of the Spirit.

55

And God was doing things. One of the joys was watching the new members unite with the church by confession and re-affirmation of faith. These were people who had moved to Burlingame and its neighbor Hillsborough (where Bing Crosby lived) because this represented the pot of gold at the end of the rainbow of the American Dream. Many found that pot empty and turned to the church for a first- or second-look. We were in a missionary situation and found great satisfaction in responding to that challenge. Another sign of God's work among us in those years was the entrance of sixteen of our youth (eight women and eight men) into the ordained ministry.

But here I am a retired minister who has been out of the pastorate for almost a quarter of a century writing in response to the expressed experience of a much younger pastor ministering in a different time and place. I do so in full recognition of the fact that my story is in no way normative for him or anyone else. I also realize that the world in which ministry is being conducted today is different in radical ways from the one I knew during my pastoral years. Yet in response to the issue that Bill Golderer has raised about what, if anything other than the CSI, confirms our call over the years following ordination, about ministerial self-understanding and sense of self-worth, I would encourage him and other young pastors to read and take seriously the apostle Paul's message of justification by faith in his Letter to the Galatians.

During my tenure at Princeton Seminary I was privileged to teach an exegesis course every other year on this epistle (the faculty trusted me with six chapters of the New Testament), and I became convinced that when the apostle speaks of "the elements of the world," as he does in chapter 4, he is referring to the same kind of realities that Pastor Golderer names the "Cultural Success Index." People who live by that index are simply attempting to justify their existence by success according to the human standards of our present culture. We ministers, however, should know better. We should know that life is not justified by human effort but by the grace of God in Jesus Christ, by that love that is unearned, undeserved, and unmerited—the same love that will never let us go, never let us down, and never let us off. Christ has freed us from that effort of self-justification, and in so doing has freed us also for the ministry of his gospel without undue regard for the success and failure standards of the CSI.

That freedom also allows us to leave the ministry for another vocation with integrity. It is simply true that our call to ministry need not be for a lifetime. As mysteriously as that call initially came it may as mysteriously depart. We may wake up one morning and realize that we do not want to do any more all the things that the ordained ministry requires of us. We may experience a crisis of faith itself. Or we may find that we are simply not able for one reason or another to do what the people of a congregation expect us to do and at the level they expect us to do it. To have that happen once may be dismissed as a bad match. But should it happen repeatedly over time it might be a sign that God is calling us to a different vocation. Our lives remain justified in Christ one way or another. God does not love us more because we are ministers or less because we are no longer or never were. Faith in this sense gives us the freedom to do something else with out lives to glorify God besides the practice of ordained ministry.

Let me now conclude with a confession. If I were fifty years younger than I am, and if God were crazy enough to call me into the ministry again, I would accept the call in a heartbeat. For despite all of the cultural changes that create new challenges for ministry in a postmodern world, pastoral ministry remains the first office of the Church and the greatest work in the world. Blessings on all of you who are engaged in doing it.

V

It's Just You and Me, God:
A Life of Prayer

David Shinn

During the second week of my summer Clinical Pastoral Education, one of my fellow interns stopped me cold in the hallway of the ICU (Intensive Care Unit) and said, "David, do you speak Chinese?" Irritated by this question, I retorted, "Just because I look Asian, doesn't necessarily mean I speak Chinese. But in this case, yes I do." Not hearing anything but my "yes," he yanked me into the pediatric neurology wing and said, "You must talk to this family!" Despite his intrusive and forceful gesture, I gazed into the room. There sat a horror-stricken Asian couple holding each other in tears over a little child with tubes coming out of his little body, covered in blood.

In the end, the family of four that came in together after a tragic accident would only leave as a family of three. That night, the father, atypical of most Asian men, broke down into sorrowful weeping. He begged me, "Tell your God that we will do anything for our younger son to be alive again! Please pray for him! Please, please, I beg you! Tell your God that for us." He pled with me as we prayed together on our knees in the Pediatric Intensive Care Unit waiting room. Hoping against all odds, we prayed for hours. In the end, the doctor pronounced the five-year-old boy brain dead.

As a father of two lively and vibrant boys reflecting on that moment of prayer, tears still stream down my face when I recall that time before God. I often wonder:

Did God really hear our prayers?

Did God care for this family?

How would I really feel about God, prayer, and all the talk about God if that were my son covered in blood?

How would you feel if you were the father or mother?

What would prayer mean to you?

What would God mean to you?

What relational connection would you have or not have, to speak to God in such a desperate time?

What the *^%$% is prayer?

Prayer is the relational conduit that connects us to God. In this chapter, I would like to partner with our Reformed theology and faith first to define what prayer is and is not. Next, I would like to share the concept and practice of blessing and cursing in our communication with our speaking God. Then combining prayer and blessing, I would like to lift up the notion that prayer is a form of blessing to God, others and self.

What is prayer? More interestingly, perhaps, let us consider what prayer is not. First, prayer is not telling God something that God otherwise would not know. Simply, God knows our hearts and words even before we conceive and utter a word. Second, prayer is not a means of forcing God to do something that God otherwise would not do.[1] Prayer is not leverage on God or a way to manipulate God. To further this point, Martin Luther points out that prayer is not for God at all. Prayer is for us. We pray, not for the effect we have on God; we pray for the effect on us. Prayer changes us, helps us, and blesses us. For in fact, prayer is the building block of the relationship we have with God. It helps us to be aware of who we are and whose we are. Through prayer, we enter into communion and covenantal relationship with God. In this

---

[1] Marcum, Walt, "Living in the Light: Leading Youth to Deeper Spirituality," (Abingdon Press, Nashville, 1994), 37.

beautiful relationship, we pray to usher blessing unto God, others and self.

Yet in speaking to and about God, others, and self, we are warned by the book of James, "From the same mouth come blessing and cursing. My brothers and sisters, this ought not to be so. Does a spring pour forth from the same opening both fresh and brackish water? Can a fig tree, my brothers and sisters, yield lives, or a grapevine figs? No more can salt water yield fresh." (James 3:10-12) The incredible struggle and reality is that from the same mouth, we have the opportunity and ability to bring a blessing or curse unto someone.

The interplay between blessing and cursing is wrapped up in the salvific plan of God for humanity. From the primeval history of Genesis 1-11, to the narrative of the Patriarchs and to the teaching of Jesus, God blesses humanity with creation, life, and covenant. Yet Adam and Eve, due to their hubris, chose curses onto themselves and upon the whole of humanity, and Cain chose murder and envy. Yet, Christ takes on the curse of sin all the way to the cross. For us, we can choose to bless or choose to curse with every word out of our mouths and every thought of our hearts.

In choosing to bless, instead of curse, new life can take place. Balaam, the hired spiritual assassin in Numbers 22, who was overwhelmed by the love of God for the Israelites and perhaps by the amazement of the talking donkey, blessed the band of riff-raff in the desert instead of cursing them. In like manner, our prayers can bring good and prosperity instead of destruction and harm. The power is ours to use.

Blessings unto God, Others, and Self

We bless God, but not because God needs our blessings. In the southern rim of the Grand Canyon, a site of breathtaking grandeur, there is a certain calm that evokes the still small voice that caught Elijah's attention in 1 Kings 19 Here lies a plaque

60

that reads, "All creation praise you O Lord." The knees weaken, hearts soften, the soul is inspired, and the mind motivated as one reads these words. For we worship a God who out of profound affection and deep love speaks the cosmos, the world, all that breathes into reality. "…'Let there be light'; and there was light … and God saw that the light was good."(Gen. 1:3-4) God spoke all that we know into being. Hovering above the pre-creation chaos, the living *Ruach*, spirit, breath of God, calls the creation into order. Such a God, who would come all the way down to be one of us, would shoulder the burden of humanity, even unto death, and only to rise to speak once more, "where O Death is your sting?" Such a God, in my opinion, would perhaps desire our blessing. Such a God would be moved by our praises and adorations. Such a God would be so touched, not that God would need any human sentimentality. More profoundly, why would such a loving God not be pleased? I am moved to consider the notion the Master of the Universe would be pleased by my little utterance of blessing: Blessings of gratitude for the first breath we inhale as we break darkness of sleep into lightness of consciousness. Blessings of deep appreciation for sharing lives, making meaning, with all those who are closest to our hearts. Blessings of deep cries when there is sorrow that no words can imitate. Blessings of deep joy that we break down when it enters our souls. Blessings that we can bring to God are profound blessings to us. In blessing, in praying, in praising, in adoring the living God, we are blessed. What a tall task that may be! Yet Edmond, who initially betrayed his siblings and Narnia to the Dark Witch blessed his brother on the eve of the battle: "Aslan believes in you, and so do I!" Prayer becomes the living force, the life to overcome death and despair.

We are blessed because we are invited into partnership, relationship, and intimacy with the Living Spirit. Such relationship and unique unity with God is not just reserved for the super spiritual praying warrior! It is for all. Thomas Merton writes:

My vocation is rare perhaps, but contemplation does not exist only within the walls of the cloister. Every man [and woman], to live a life full of significance, is called simply to know the significant interior of life and to find ultimate significance in its proper inscrutable existence, in spite of himself [and herself], in spite of the world and appearance, in the Living God.[2]

For Merton, this first step is crucial. We must turn to God and acknowledge our relationship with God and turn toward the true self as God intends. Our hearts call us to return to the source of All Reality to know our true identity. We are so richly blessed when we awaken to our relationship regularly and daily. What is more marvelous, we bring blessing to our loving God. We turn inward to discover once again who we really are. It is a blissful journey of self-discovery full of renunciation of who we are not, and toward the path of transformation to who we can become. For Christ, our living savior has given himself for the sake of humanity. In the movie, *Narnia*, the great lion Aslan is bound, and as such he offers himself to the witch. He doesn't fight back as he undergoes the further humiliation, of being shorn of his magnificent mane, and with it the great title, King of Beasts. As the witch announces victory over all beasts by promising her sovereignty over Narnia, she strikes her spear deep into Aslan. Aslan has given his life to save Edmond. The story could end here. But we know that more is to come. Transformation must happen from within so we can go outward toward others. Prayer is the very stone that supports the path of our journey.

Merton, seeing the world in suffering, seeing the transformation in himself, changed to bring transformation to

---

[2] From <u>Honorable Reader: Reflection on My Work</u> by Thomas Merton, edited by Robert E. Daggy (Crossroad, 1989), p. 39. Used by permission of the Merton Legacy Trust.

others. His inner journey was only the beginning for the outward journey. Our inner journey into prayer leads us to outward journey. For we dare to believe that as, like the little band of disciples before us believed, we can bring changes to the world. By participating, giving, offering, and lifting our prayers, we too can affect change.

"Prayer is an expression ... speaking to God from the bottoms of our hearts,"[3] Long writes. Perhaps the God who speaks the world into creation is the God who desires to hear our prayer as we begin each day. Long continues: "God calls to each of us, calls us from sleep, calls us to get up and be human, to live toward joy, to put one foot in front of the other this day as one who belongs to God ... among the first human acts we do each day is to imitate God by opening our mouths and speaking. God speaks the creation into being, we respond to God's voice with our own" by praying. In that posture of prayer, we can fully be honest. Even in the hardest of times, even in our most profound loss, even in our wildest anger, we can bring it all to God. With full honesty, with full integrity, with full truth of our heart, we bring it all to God in blessing and prayer.

Merton moves us inward to our true self, and guides us outward to the world. From our true inner self, we can begin moving outward. The blessings we receive from the saving Christ, bless us and bring inner transformation and thus the transformation of the world. With the river of blessing, we can pray and bless others. Yet we stand once again in the balancing act of teetering one way to bless or teetering another way to curse others. In choosing to pray for the needs and concerns for others, we can usher the blessing of God to flow into and out of our lives. Watching our fractured and broken world, the true self in us must speak. Perhaps with similar power and opportunity as when God calls the creation into order from chaos, we dare to

---

[3] Tom Long, Testimony: Talking Ourselves into Being Christian (San Francisco: Jossey-Bass), 99. Reprinted with permission of John Wiley & Sons, Inc.

believe that our prayers can move, change, transform, and bless the world of pain into comfort. We do not live alone; we are, in fact, created for the community and family of God. Such community transcends beyond geographical, temporal, physical, metaphysical realms. God creates the world for good. Yet it is fractured with brokenness and we are ambassadors to call the world back to awareness of the radical reality of God in it. Craig Rennobolm, the mental health chaplain of my current congregation, works tirelessly with the homeless population in Seattle. He once noted in his training seminar the incredible capacity of the human heart to care. We feel pain in our hearts when we see someone suffering, though the terror and pain of suffering are not our own. Suffering is universal, but it is not God's intended creation. Our hearts, tuned to God's heartbeat, can detect the disharmony and seek to bring harmony by praying for transformation, praying for the end of genocide and civil war in Darfur, praying for justice and civil rights for the millions of undocumented immigrants in our country, praying for a family bereft of their son. We pray for others to bring blessing unto their lives and to engage them directly, personally and spiritually.

"Does a spring pour forth from the same opening both fresh and brackish water?" (James 3:11) Of course not. We can bring blessing to God by praising God for God's creation. We can bring blessing to others when we stand in solidarity with them with prayer. We can bless ourselves by engaging God and by walking with and supporting others. In doing so, our lives are enriched and blessed. Let our lives be like a living prayer.

Response by Lonnie Oliver
to David Shinn on Prayer

Does God answer prayer?

During the Civil Rights Movement the marchers prayed before they marched to face billy clubs, dogs, and water hoses from policemen and firemen. As they prayed and marched and prayed as they marched they believed that God answered their prayers for victory, peace, grace, and strength.

I agree with Derrick Bell, who said:

> The power of prayer has carried black people over troubled waters, through valleys of dry bones, through paths of blood and tears. Prayer has been our cry for freedom and deliverance—both a supplication and celebration.[1]

Persons who believe that God answers prayer tend to believe the impossible, comprehend the incomprehensible, attempt great things for God, and believe that the Lord will make a way somehow.

If African-Americans didn't believe that God answers prayer, they would not have spent so much time opening themselves up to God. They would not have spent so much time trying to experience the presence of God. We should understand that God answers prayer in

---

[1] From Derrick Bell's review of the book, Standing in the Need of Prayer: A Celebration of Black Prayer by the Schomburg Center for Research in Black Culture (New York: Free Press, 2003). Reprinted with permission.

many different ways based on God's will and God's purpose.

We need to understand what prayer is. In prayer, we enter into a relationship with God to be transformed by God. It is a sharing with the divine nature. It is dialogue with God and being aware of God's presence. In other words, prayer is a life-style of being aware of God's presence so that we can serve as a power with God by participating in Kingdom-building activities.

Prayer is a faith-strengthening activity. Listen to the Heidelberg Catechism:

> Q/A.116.   Why is prayer necessary for Christians?
> *"Because it is the chief part of the gratitude which God requires of us and because God will give his grace and Holy Spirit only to those who sincerely beseech him in prayer without ceasing, and who thank Him for these gifts."*[2]

Prayer allows us to be empowered to live the Christian life and to rely upon God's grace and mercy.

Prayer changes our attitude toward God. As we pray, we come to see that God is the Divine Lover who hears our cries and whose will is for our wholeness and well-being. Prayer helps us to understand that God loves us and that God is a personal God who wants the best for us. In other words, to know that God answers prayer, we need a Theology of Prayer. Our prayer should be God-centered. The purpose of prayer is to praise and glorify God.   Our prayers are not designed to make God understand us but to help us understand God. We have

---

[2] Reprinted with permission of the Office of the General Assembly, Presbyterian Church (U.S.A.).

been called to seek God's will and not our will. We should strive not to get God to do our bidding but to change our ways to do God's bidding.

Prayer is not just to get things from God or petition God for our wants; but we should see prayer as an excellent opportunity to converse with God. Communion with God through prayer is a joyful opportunity. When we are in communion with God through prayer we seek not merely to gain something from God, but to be in relationship with God. When we cultivate a relationship with and through prayer, we grow spiritually and mature in our faith.

A Theology of Prayer includes opportunities to renew a sense of God's presence through self-examination. We should always pray and ask the Holy Spirit to convict us of areas in our lives that need transformation and repentance. A self-examined life will help us to become more faithful and obedient to God's will. Prayer is needed so that we can hear God's voice in ways that will motivate us to seek God's grace and mercy or even to let go of our self and allow God's Spirit to transform us. A Theology of Prayer allows time and space for confession.

A Theology of Prayer involves solitude and meditation. Prayer requires finding moments to be alive with God and laying aside our worldly thoughts and concerns. It allows us to hear and experience God's presence in different ways. This type of prayer fixes our mind and soul on God, the scriptures, images, pictures, and words or symbols of the faith.

One symbol that helps me to connect with God and have conversation with God is a West African Akan spiritual symbol:

GYE NYAME ("Except God")

It is a symbol that has several interpretations. "Except God" simply means that one recognizes the supremacy of God and, in essence, that one is not afraid of anything—except the Supreme Being. One should always have confidence in one's ability to do things and should not be hindered from doing anything except what God forbids.

Gye Nyame also means that one recognizes that God is omnipotent and omnipresent, that God is above all. The Supreme Being is the creator of the world and all things that are in it. The Supreme Being controls all things in the world as well as the powers that operate within this world. This symbol helps me to realize that God answers prayer.

Prayer is not only solitude and meditation. It involves addressing issues of justice—praying—praying and acting in prophetic ways for the oppressed and poor.

Based on my understanding of prayer, a Theology of Prayer and my experiences with prayer, I believe that God answers prayer.

"And this is the boldness we have in him, that if we ask anything according to his will, he hears us."
(1 John 5:14)

VI

Preaching Without a Pulpit or Robe

Jud Hendrix

My father who is a long time preacher (hear "long time" in a positive "wisdom" sense) recently preached at our church. During the sermon he asked an interesting question to the congregation.

"For the rest of your life, if you could only hear sermons preached or only take communion, which would you choose?"

When he asked the congregation to raise their hands, there were only two who chose sermons. Two people! Out of the seventy or so people gathered, only two would choose to hear sermons, neither of whom were my Co-Pastor or myself. Even we preachers would choose celebrating communion over hearing a sermon. Of course our reformed tradition does not allow us to separate "proclaimed word" and "sacrament" so clearly, but the response of the congregation still seems significant. What is going on here?

Preaching for me is an increasingly odd and ambiguous task of ordained ministry. Even after hearing, or maybe even giving a "good sermon" I am often left wondering, *What just happened here? Was that even helpful? Was that worth the time?* Our community's response to my father's question points to a variety of challenges facing us as a new generation of preachers seeking to live out our call to be ministers of Word and Sacrament.

In this chapter I hope to address some of the challenges of preaching in this time of cultural change and transition as the church emerges once again with new wine skins for the transformative Spirit of God. I would like to explore what it would look like to preach without a pulpit or a robe.

Preaching Without A Pulpit

The church I serve, along with many other emerging churches, is seeking to connect with those who are disconnected from the church, those who have become de-churched. Here is one of the challenges they present to us: *We can no longer assume that the community we serve will participate in a corporate worship service as their primary spiritual practice.* Since Covenant Community does not have a building and many of our participants do not attend worship, my co-pastor and I spend a significant amount of time seeking to teach and proclaim the gospel through alternative modalities. So here is the opportunity presented to us: *We need to cultivate skills and tools in new and alternative ways of teaching and proclaiming the gospel that are not primarily dependent upon participation in a traditional worship service.*

Of course our Reformed theology and our *Book of Order* both affirm and make space for a variety of ways to "proclaim" the gospel. However, our seminary training and the reigning professional and cultural norms for pastors still assume we will spend ten to fifteen hours preparing a weekly sermon for public worship. In light of the emerging North American context and the cultivation of alternative faith communities that are not primarily based on a corporate worship experience, this norm needs to be deconstructed and reconsidered. This is not a call to completely replace preaching behind a pulpit during a service of worship. Instead it is a call to expand our modalities of proclamation. Reformed worship, with its deep and wonderful tradition of pulpit preaching, needs to be affirmed and included as we move into the future. But it should also be expanded and transcended to include other modalities of public proclamation.

The opportunity here is to allow the spirit of the gospel to be proclaimed through the entirety of our lives as they are lived out in the world. Proclamation can occur through our encounters and conversations at bars, coffee shops, and school PTA meetings. It can happen through joining community boards, neighborhood meetings and having friends in our homes. Proclamation in these spaces will require new interpretive frameworks, new theological commentaries and new skills in different modalities of communication.

How can we deepen our understanding of proclamation and expand our proclamation tools to include other forms of faithful conversation and spiritual direction that happen outside the walls of the church? What preaching "postures" are needed when we move outside the walls of the church into the world? Maybe in our preaching classes we should video ourselves at bars and coffee shops just as we do behind pulpits, so we can become mindful of our mannerisms, subtle forms of communication, and word usage in those places of witness and proclamation.

The assumption of having a traditional pulpit behind which to preach is being questioned as new ecclesiological models and new forms of pastoral ministry emerge. The good news is that new pulpits are popping up all over the place, but they will require a new set of communication skills and a commitment to renewed creativity.

Preaching Without A Robe

Kris Delmhorst creatively presents the challenge of preaching to a postmodern context in her song, "Yellow Brick Road." She proclaims:

> *I'm off to see the wizard in his castle on the hill,*
> *and I never once have known him,*
> *and I do not know him still*

his face is magnificent, but you will never see his hands
and the way he throws his voice around
I don't know where he stands
I am off to see the wizard with his curtain and his crown.
but my hands are not trembling, my head it is not bowed
because I am not looking for any answers,
no truths to be revealed.
all that I am asking is to show me something real

Cause, I am not on no yellow break road
got a mind and a heart and guts of my own
I am not looking for a one to set me free
I am not on no yellow brick road
I find my own way home
I am just looking for someone to walk with me.[1]

In her song, Delmhorst reflects a deep-seated impression of many professional preachers. We hide our true selves behind our *pulpits* and *stoles—the* ecclesial equivalent of *curtain* and *crown*. Preachers often stand in pulpits like *the wizard in his castle on the hill*. Yet, as Delmhorst proclaims, her hands are not trembling, her head is not bowed. She is not looking for any answers, or truths to be revealed. She has a mind, a heart and guts of her own and does not need our rational truths to set her free. Delmhorst reflects several important characteristics of our emerging postmodern culture. *Authority in our emerging context comes not from ecclesial position or from the ordainments of tradition, or the ability to proclaim rational propositional truths, but instead authority comes from authenticity, transparency and holistic embodiment of the transformative Spirit of God.*

Instead of a traditional preacher hiding behind intuitional masks and rational words many are looking for an

---

[1] Lyrics from "Yellow Brick Road" by Kris Delmhorst (Big Bean Music) from Album: "Five Stories" (Catalyst Disc/Signature Sounds Recording Company). Reprinted with permission.

authentic embodiment of a transformed life that is revealed through a holistic journey in community. Even when this includes traditional preaching and teaching, the *way* in which we preach and teach needs to be more holistic, engaging the full person—body, mind, soul and spirit. In my estimation the art of preaching is dying because it is no longer understood as a form of art, but instead a task and a responsibility of ordained ministry. Preaching has become limited to a stimulating lecture for the brain, rather than an experience for the whole person. The gospel that we are called to proclaim is not primarily a set of rational words and thoughts that we introduce to minds of our congregants for their acceptance and understanding. The gospel is instead a transformative process that brings about healing and wholeness for the whole individual, which means it should evoke and stimulate all of our senses and ways of being. At times the gospel does flow from words and thoughts, but it also flows from emotions, sounds, images, subtle energies and fleshy touch. How many of these aspects of humanity are addressed in the traditional act of preaching?

The gospel of John says it well "The word became flesh and dwelt among us." We Presbyterians, being somewhat uncomfortable with our own flesh, decided we would try to reduce it back to words again. The popular quote by St. Francis of Assisi states the challenge clearly, "Proclaim the gospel at all times, and if necessary use words."

Our hiding behind professional preacher personas and using rational words and thought as the primary modality of our preaching often hides the incarnating word of God that is becoming flesh within the totality of our lives. The embodied gospel, which we are called to preach, is weaved in and through the entirely of our bodies and lives and is most fully shared as we journey together as whole people. Our proclamation cannot be separated from the core of our being, because the "core of our being" is the locale of the gospel.

73

Listen to the words of the Suffi poet, Rumi:

... but come!
Take a pick-axe
and break apart
your stony self

the heart's matrix is glutted with rubies,
springs of laughter are buried in your breast,

unstop the wine jar,
batter down the door to the treasury of nonexistence

the water in your jug is brackish and low,
smash the jug and come to the river![2]

The call to embody proclamation with our whole lives is frightening because it requires us to be authentic and transparent with our whole selves. In light of the responsibility of this calling, we can all say, like the wizard in Delmhorst's song, "but there is no one here but me." At this point our communities will rejoice in their response, "but who did you think we came here to see?" Our communities want to see a transformed life, not a professional persona.

This call to transparency and authenticity in our proclamation is not a call to preach ourselves, or for the preacher to be the subject of the proclamation. Instead it is an invitation to "full person preaching" where we journey with others into the transformative locale of the gospel which is everywhere—around us, in us and through us—all of us. We are called and equipped to proclaim not because we are officially sanctioned by

---

[2] From <u>The Rumi Collection: An Anthology of Translations of Mevlana Jalaluddin Rumi</u> selected and edited by Kabir Helminski, © 1998 by Kabir Helminski. Reprinted by arrangement with Shambhala Publications, Inc., Boston, MA. www.shambhala.com.

the ecclesial authorities, but because the transformative power of God has reached the core of our being which is "glutted with rubies" and "springs of laughter."

I understand better now why my congregation would rather take communion than hear a sermon. Communion is an embodied and multi-sensory experience that feels more communal than most sermons. During communion we become companions on a journey rather than wizards in a castle. Maybe the sacramental side of our pastoral identity can shed some light on our preaching side. As we look more closely and creatively at our assumptions and interpretation of what it means to be a preacher in a postmodern world, maybe our understanding of the sacraments can be a guide and help.

Preaching without a pulpit and a robe leaves us naked on the street—interesting new preaching postures for the postmodern pastor.

Response by Thomas W. Gillespie
to Jud Hendrix on Preaching

There is much in what Jud Hendrix writes that is worthy of strong affirmation. I share his concern that Christian proclamation ought to show what Kris Delmhorst calls "something real," indeed, "someone to walk with me." I agree that authority in our post-modern context will not be recognized in "ecclesial position" or "the ordainments of tradition," or even in "rational propositional truths."

I, too, think pastoral preaching should be "an experience for the whole person" and not merely "a stimulating lecture for the brain." I am all for "authenticity, transparency and holistic embodiment" of the message in the messenger. And I could not care less what the preacher wears or where he or she stands when preaching. Beyond that, however, we have issues that merit discussion.

Jud's reference to his pastor father asking his congregation which they would prefer for the rest of their lives, listening to sermons or celebrating communion, brought to mind something I heard my own father say many years ago. At the time we were members of a rather dynamic Presbyterian church in Southern California and our pastor was a charismatic preacher in the best sense of that word. With reference to that Sunday morning event, my Dad said one day, "When our minister enters the sanctuary to lead worship he has a look on his face that says, 'I have discovered something exciting in the gospel this week, and if you are not good I will not tell you." Now that is expectation! And even more so coming from a blue collar union activist without a college degree. My father would have voted for preaching, at least of that kind, over communion any day, although being of Scottish immigrant descent the

76

Lord's Table was by him greatly revered. What my father said was true not only for him but for our entire congregation, including myself as a teenager. Long before I arrived at Princeton Theological Seminary and learned of Karl Barth, Emil Brunner, and Rudolf Bultmann, I knew from my personal experience about "God's ability to work in the moment through the Word." I did not have to wait until I was in a doctoral seminar at Claremont Graduate School to hear about the *Wortgeschehen* (Gerhard Ebeling) and *Sprachereignis* (Ernst Fuchs). The "Word event" was already a decisive part of my Christian life. For I met the *reality* of God's redeeming love in Jesus Christ in and through that kind of preaching.

Many years later, as a pastor of a Presbyterian church on the San Francisco Peninsula, I found myself one night in the coffee shop at the International Airport with a group of fellow ministers visiting with a revered pastor who was leaving his church in order to accept a professorship in ministry at a theological seminary. In the course of our conversation he said, "I really do not know why I am doing this, because we do not learn ministry in seminary but from the significant pastors we have known." That rankled me. My seminary experience had been very positive, and I was convinced in that moment that it was at Princeton that I had learned ministry. As I went through the following week, however, I found myself asking why preaching, theological study, and pastoral care were decisive for me in what I was doing. And to my great surprise, I could attribute each to one of my own pastors while growing up in the church. There is not doubt in my mind that my understanding of preaching was shaped during those formative years when our pastor walked into the sanctuary on a Sunday morning with a look on his face that said, "I have discovered something exciting in God's Word this week, and if you are not good I will not tell you."

What made his preaching exciting was not his personal charm and warmth of personality, although that was certainly a human factor, but *his* expectation that when he proclaimed the gospel of Jesus Christ the message would be used by the Holy Spirit to make a redemptive difference in the lives of those who heard it. This was nothing new, however. The apostle Paul shared that same expectation when he preached the gospel. To the Corinthians he wrote these words about the Christian ministry and preaching:

> Therefore, since it is by God's mercy that we are engaged in this ministry, we do not lose heart. We have renounced the shameful things that one hides; we refuse to practice cunning or to falsify God's word; but by the open statement of the truth we commend ourselves to the conscience of every one in the sight of God. And even if our gospel is veiled, it is veiled to those who are perishing. In their case the god of this world has blinded the minds of the unbelievers, to keep them from seeing the light of the gospel of the glory of Christ, who is the image of God. For we do not proclaim ourselves; we proclaim Jesus Christ as Lord and ourselves as your slaves for Jesus' sake. For it is the God who said, 'Let light shine out of darkness', who has shone in our hearts to give the light of the knowledge of the glory of God in the face of Jesus Christ.
>
> (2 Corinthians 4:1-6)

There is authenticity and transparency and embodiment of ministry in that statement, and through the preaching that emerges from it occurs nothing less than a *Christophany.* Paul speaks of "the light of the gospel of the glory of Christ, who is the image of God." It is the "glory of Christ" that glows through the gospel to illumine human life. It is the God who called forth light in the world who also shines in human hearts and gives "the light of the knowledge of the glory of God in the face of Jesus Christ."

With reference to this Corinthian passage, the German New Testament scholar Peter Stuhlmacher contends that the Christian sermon is a "word-room." By that he means the sermon creates an intelligible and sensible space by the use of human words that bear witness to Jesus Christ, who by his presence through the Spirit fills that room and demonstrates to the hearer that the sermon is not empty talk. Put simply, through the sermon we do not merely hear something (although that is a necessary factor) but we meet the One attested (that is the redemptive factor). So long as that happens, it does not matter where preachers stand or what they wear when they proclaim the gospel. Equally irrelevant is where they are not standing or what they are not wearing if Christ is not manifested in their preaching.

Shortly before leaving our congregation in Burlingame, California, for the presidency at Princeton Seminary, my wife and I traveled with some forty of our church members on one of those "In the Footsteps of St. Paul" tours of Greece. Our visit to ancient Corinth left an indelible impression on me. Standing there in the *agora* (marketplace) we looked at the *bema* (preaching stone) where rhetoricians stood to proclaim their respective political or philosophical or religious message to anyone who would listen. I found myself imagining this little Jewish messenger of the gospel standing there on that very stone and, as he later put it, preaching "Christ crucified" (1 Cor. 1:23) to a pre-modern audience that was in so many ways like their future post-modern counterparts. Corinth was a hot bed of ethnic diversity, religious pluralism, and philosophical relativity. How in the world did the preaching of Paul ever create a church in Corinth? Looking back on that initial encounter from the *bema*, he gave this answer:

79

When I came to you, brothers and sisters,
I did not come proclaiming the mystery
of God to you in lofty words or wisdom.
For I decided to know nothing among
you except Jesus Christ, and him crucified.
And I came to you in weakness and
in fear and in much trembling.
My speech and my proclamation were not with
plausible words of wisdom,
but with a demonstration of the Spirit and of power,
so that your faith might rest not on human wisdom
but on the power of God.

(1 Corinthians 2:1-5)

It remains my conviction that if Paul's proclamation of the gospel as a human act could create a church in ancient Corinth because the Spirit of God used it to create faith in "Jesus Christ, and him crucified" among his hearers in the *agora*, the preaching of the same Christ will create and sustain and correct and guide a church in our time as well, postmodern or otherwise, and by the same Spirit.

But it must be Christ Jesus who is proclaimed in order for the Spirit to manifest him to the auditors as real and reliable. Preaching from a biblical text is insufficient. For one could preach from the bible over a forty-year ministry and never once preach the gospel of Jesus Christ. The bible is important as the initial and, yes, authoritative witness of the Church and the Spirit to Jesus, but we are called to preach Christ as biblically attested, not simply the bible. I find this to be an important, even crucial distinction. Jesus himself *is* the gospel. The bible bears its witness to him as such. And we Christian preachers today are called to preach Jesus as good news to postmodern people who are indeed looking for something real, perhaps even someone who will walk with them.

I realize that this will sound odd if not worse to some readers, even as it seemed odd to one of my elders in my first church, a new church development in Southern California. He drove up one Saturday morning as I was mowing the lawn and we visited there on the grass. He was the chair of our fledgling Christian Education Committee and thus familiar with the Presbyterian Sunday School curriculum of that time. Called the *Faith and Life Series*, it was based on a three year cycle that began with Jesus Christ as the theme in year one, focused on the bible in year two, and concluded with a year on the church. We were in the second year of our ministry there and he wanted to know why I was still preaching every Sunday about Jesus rather than the Bible. I was at first perplexed by the question because I knew of nothing else to preach. Then it dawned on me that this man had never before been in a church where Christ was the constant theme of preaching. I say that without a trace of judgment on his previous pastors and equally without breaking my arm patting myself on the back. It is merely a statement of fact, but an important one. For I do not think the church today can thrive in its postmodern milieu by focusing either on itself or on the bible. Neither carry much weight in our contemporary American society. The preacher can no longer say, "The Church teaches...," or "The Bible says ..." and expect to be convincing thereby. But we can and must point to Jesus Christ who is the reality of God for us, the Christ who manifests himself in and through human proclamation that has him as its subject matter, the Christ in whom the Spirit creates faith, the Christ in whose face we are given "the light of the knowledge of the glory of God."

It is this emphasis that I find missing from Jud Hendrix's otherwise fine essay. In fact the name of Jesus Christ does not appear in what he has written, much less as the unique subject of Christian preaching. I am sure that is an oversight on his part, but it is a dangerous oversight. For Christian preaching does not depend upon such matters as where preachers stand or what they wear when they preach. It does depend upon what or whom they preach. So I say to my young colleague in ministry and others of his generation, preach from wherever you need to and wear whatever you can get away with when you do, but preach Jesus Christ at all times and in all places. That will grow a church—even, No, especially in a postmodern time.

VII

Stale Bread & Sour Wine: Keeping the Gospel Real Through the Sacraments

Neal D. Presa

> Dry wafer,
> sour wine.
>
> This day I see
>   God's in the dust,
>   not sifted
>   out from confusion.
>
> Dry wafer,
>   sour wine:
>   this day I see
>   the world, a word
>   intricately incarnate, offers –
>   raveled, honeycombed, veined, stained
>   what hunger craves,
>   a sorrel grass,
>   a crust,
>   water,
>   salt.
>
> —Denise Levertov, "This Day"[1]

---

[1] By Denise Levertov, from OBLIQUE PRAYERS, copyright © 1984 by Denise Levertov. Reprinted by permission of New Directions Publishing Corp.

A community can and does teach one another. A community can even teach their pastor a thing or two. I'm not talking about those endless debates at Session meetings that leave minds twisted and churned, nor the Bible study sessions that produce more questions than "Aha!" moments. Rather, I am talking about a lesson given by a genuine Word delivered not from a prepared manuscript, but proclaimed right from the pew during the sealing of the Word.

Just when we preacher-types thought our time in the pulpit, in front of the baptismal font, or behind the Lord's Table were holy places for only holy people, where we decide whether to say or sing the *Sursum Corda*, and whether to use the Great Prayer of Thanksgiving (version D) from the *Book of Common Worship* or some other lectionary source, we follow a long line of prophets and priests in holding the activities of the chancel area as our territory. After all, the thinking goes, it takes someone ordained trained at a seminary with an M.Div. or a B.D.; someone who has taken those ords, answered questions from the Committee on Preparation for Ministry and the Committee on Ministry; all this candidates for ministry undergo in order to repeat the Words of Institution, to tear the bread, pour the juice, splash the water, and utter the Trinitarian formula. Are our liturgical, pastoral, theological, exegetical bubbles filled without warrant?

Consider that our own *Book of Order* grants five, yes, five "powers" to pastors that are neither under the jurisdiction of the Session nor require its consent. We have the enviable authority to select the Scripture text to be read (yes, no apologies owed to the lectors for having them read from the census of the Book of Numbers!); to prepare and preach the sermon; to prepare and offer prayers in worship and elsewhere; to select music and hymns, and to choose to use drama or another art form in worship. [2]

There's something wrong with a theological education system, a pastoral-ecclesial system, and a congregational setting in which the expectation is that the one holy catholic apostolic Church bestows all theological/liturgical lessons upon the minister through the seminary, governing body, Calvin's *Institutes*, James White's *Brief Introduction to Worship, Book of Common Worship*. Sure, we can have worship committees to guide and consult on liturgical matters. But the default responsibility falls upon the one(s) who are specially trained and equipped to minister with "energy, intelligence, imagination, and love."[2] Such a widespread portrait distorts the communal responsibility of every member of the priesthood of all believers to mutually enrich one another in order to fulfill our baptismal commitments to worship and serve God to the fullest. And while we might take steps to create a feeling of more lay participation in liturgical planning or re-arrange the pews and add more antiphons to the worship bulletin to develop a "community feel," these are only steps. What is called for are leaps … leaps to enable the community to truly live into what it means to be a *koinonia* of the Acts 2:42-44/post-Pentecost type.

I serve a small congregation in central New Jersey. When I was called here almost five years ago, this community prided itself on being one of the first churches in the area to have "contemporary praise songs" complete with a "praise band," overhead projector with screen, with accompanying charismatic/spontaneous prayers throughout at the second worship service at 10:30 a.m.

Then there's the first worship service at 8:00 a.m.[3] This service has an average attendance of twelve worshipers (in the summers, sometimes as few as five), who have resisted

---

[2] The Constitution of the Presbyterian Church (U.S.A.), Part II, The Book of Order, 2005-2007. (Louisville: Office of the General Assembly, 2005), G-14.0207h.

[3] As of September 2007, the 8:00 a.m. and the 10:30 a.m. worship services merged to a 9:30 a.m. service, in which the Eucharist is celebrated every Sunday, and there is a mixture of traditional hymns and contemporary Christian music.

combining with the second and have put up a fight against uniting both services during special occasions. This 8:00 a.m. service has gone on for eons, celebrating the Lord's Supper every Sunday. There are no "contemporary praise songs"; hymnals are a must (the red one), and written, liturgical rubrics are welcome. Truth be told, this was the very first battle I found myself in within the first month of this call: the 8am-ers vs. the 10:30am-ers vs. the unifiers.

Spontaneity, liveliness and mischief are actually the orders of the day at the 8:00 a.m. service every Sunday since I've been a pastor. Not because of the band, because there is none. Not because of songs by Casting Crowns or Nicole Nordeman. Nope, you won't find their voices there. We sing Isaac Watts, Fanny Crosby, and Charles Wesley, thank you very much. And not because of me.

I have springtime pollen allergies. The season from March through June wreaks havoc on my sinuses and on the Kleenex supply. And so it was on that April morning when I was leading the congregational prayers prior to the celebration of the Supper. I caught in my peripheral vision the waving hand of one of our energetic deacons, Linda.[4] She kept waving … more like swatting. I continued with the prayers. At the Table the congregation and I went through the Eucharistic liturgy. Somehow the Distribution of Elements seems to provide the arena for the unplanned, unsolicited, but wholesome pastor-parish-*koinonia* relationship. On this Sunday morning, the frustrated deacon who had all this time unsuccessfully attempted to get my attention with her swatting/waving/karate-chopping hands decided to seize the opportunity. Rather than taking a generous portion of the consecrated bread she decided to place her index finger and thumb into my right nostril and

---

[4] Deacon Linda Makowski died during the editing of this manuscript. I recounted this humorous encounter at her funeral service.

86

pluck a piece of tissue lint that had been dangling there to her irritation (and to my consternation)!

There was something honest about that gesture, I mused later. It was real. It was a no-holds-barred, unashamedly non-liturgical in the traditional sense, but very liturgical and sacramental in the family sense. It was something that my aunts would have done, or even my cousins. It is what family does.

I think of Evelyn, one of our darling widows, a fellow 8am-er. As an octogenarian, she knows she can get away with anything, and she says so. She's one who has enjoyed life, who speaks her mind, who will freely talk about sex to you inside and outside church, who wishes she could drive a sports car, and who does not hold back from chiding those with multiple "prayer requests" as "complainers." With about twelve to fifteen people attending the 8:00 a.m. service, I invite all worshippers to come forward to the front during the Eucharist; and while I usually have the 8am-ers serve the elements to one another, when I get to Nancy, Evelyn, Helen, and Barbara, I hold onto the paten (the plate) and cup. Three of these four widows, who are always right next to each other can't stand for too long a period of time. Evelyn's comments to Helen cover the gamut as she passes the bread. Here's a sampling of her quotable quips at various times at the Table:

> "Now, don't take too much"
> "Don't be greedy, just a pinch"
> "Wow, this is hard. I can't pull it. This must be frozen. Be careful you might break your teeth"
> "I know" (*upon hearing the words, "Evelyn, this is the body of Christ given for you"*)
> "Shall we go on a date?" (*to me*)

There's something liberating and authentic about the 8:00 a.m. family. They combine the freedom of spontaneity and gaiety with the tethering of the liturgical and creedal foundations of the

Church to ground us to the past. There's a wholesome, holistic experience of doing the Eucharist together and we are left, in the end, to say, "Thank you, God." Thank you for each other. Thank you for gifting us with each other. Thank you for Jesus. That's what the Eucharist is, isn't it? Literally a meal of "thanksgiving."

And so, I thank God for the 8am-ers. They are on the cutting-edge, not fearing to learn and certainly not fearing to teach. They embody for me what the late Fr. Alexander Schmemann of the Russian Orthodox Church called "liturgical theology," finding the source and origin of the Church's theology right in its liturgical action. In contrast to Schmemann's context of a liturgical theology that is localized in the formalism of the Orthodox Church's Eucharistic celebration, I find the incarnational element of the 8am-ers refreshing. One senses in this celebration an earthiness reminiscent of Jesus, with dusty feet in sandals, a dirty robe from his itinerant travels, eating simple foods, dining with sinners, without pretension or ostentation, neither high in the mountain or in the towers of the theological school, but down in the valley, in the towns, where the blind man, the outcasts, the hemorrhaging woman, the merchants are.

Schmemann, and those who presently continue his agenda of liturgical theology in varying forms,[5] call the Church

---

[5] Schmemann's seminal work on the matter is Introduction to Liturgical Theology (Paris: YMCA Press, 1961). For successive works on liturgical theology see Theologia Prima: What is Liturgical Theology? 2d ed. by David Fagerberg (Chicago: Hillenbrand Books, 2004); On Liturgical Theology by Aidan Kavanagh (Collegeville, MN: Liturgical Press, 1992); Primary Sources of Liturgical Theology: A Reader by Dwight Vogel (Collegeville, MN: Liturgical Press, 2000); Worship as Meaning: A Liturgical Theology for Late Modernity by Graham Hughes (Cambridge University Press, 2003); Wise and Discerning Hearts: An Introduction to Wisdom Liturgical Theology by Jill Crainshaw (Collegeville, MN: Liturgical Press, 2000); Anamnesis as Dangerous Memory: Political and Liturgical Theology in Dialogue by Bruce Morrill (Collegeville, MN: Liturgical Press, 2000); Gordon Lathrop's trilogy – Holy Things: A Liturgical Theology (Augsburg Fortress Publishers, 1995), Holy People: A Liturgical Ecclesiology (Augsburg Fortress Publishers, 1999), Holy Ground: A

to see that theology at its most helpful is not some abstract exercise, using categories imported from the outside, developed by theologians, and then applied to the Church to evaluate worship (theology of worship). Rather, the worshipping community shapes the Church's belief (*lex credendi*) as it is unearthed there through the acts of God's community (lex orandi). In short hand, *lex orandi* is *lex credendi*, the Church's worship is primary theology and thus serves as the main criterion to evaluate the degree of cohesion and coherence of the Church's life and belief.

Liturgical theology is a treasure that will enable the Church to recapture the Acts 2:42-44/post-Pentecost portrait of our early Church forbearers. Taken at its best, for us Reformed folk liturgical theology upholds both God's sovereignty and human responsibility: God acting in and through the Church, as the Church responds to God's act. What we call worship, the late Roman Catholic liturgical theologian Aidan Kavanagh calls "adjustment." The Church's worship is the act of adjusting as a response to God's revelation to Christ's gathered community.

Even though our 8am-ers have never heard of liturgical theology and probably would roll their eyes if I even mentioned it, they are engaged in liturgical theology. Theology must be allowed to be expressed, articulated and observed while the worship happens. This is distinct from "studying" worship, examining it with predetermined theological categories after the worship event has been completed and the community was blessed and dismissed. The 8am-ers are doing theology in the midst of the Eucharist, they are teaching each other, and they are definitely teaching me. They combine the appreciation and

---

Liturgical Cosmology (Augsburg Fortress Publishers, 2003); Worship as Theology: Foretaste of Glory Divine by Don Saliers (Nashville: Abingdon Press, 1994); Doxology: The Praise of God in Worship, Doctrine, and Life A Systematic Theology by Geoffrey Wainwright (New York: Oxford University Press, 1984); Context and Text: Method in Liturgical Theology by Kevin Irwin (Collegeville, MN: Liturgical Press, 1994).

embodiment of the richness of past tradition, and the creation of contemporary stories to continue that tradition with their own. They bring the pedestrian living of the suburbs, with the honest-to-goodness struggles of all frail, imperfect, sinful human beings—and they aren't afraid to say so!

Generational shifts reveal the varying patterns of both rejection and reception of the Eucharistic tradition. The World War II generation ("the greatest generation") lived during a time when Christianity and Christendom were the mainstays of American life. All things Christian were accepted, and tradition was highly valued. The Baby-Boomers reacted against denomination, authority, hierarchy, and tradition, choosing not to belong to the Church, or even to oppose the Church. Parallel to these societal and cultural developments was the convening of the Second Vatican Council, which took major strides in bringing the liturgical life of the Roman Catholic Church a bit closer to the laity.[6] Two decades later, the World Council of Churches issued *Baptism, Eucharist, and Ministry*, a major ecumenical study paper that reiterated liturgical, apostolic tradition but called the church to contextualize its practices.

The Generation X (born after about 1964) finds meaning in multiple things, enjoys the ambiguous, establishes significance in community and in the process of being community, and is comfortable with importing meanings from traditions, while interpreting and re-interpreting them to fit their

---

[6] Constitution on the Sacred Liturgy *Sacro Sanctum Concilium* promulgated by Pope Paul VI in 1963 had as its purpose the following: "This sacred Council has several aims in view: it desires to impart an ever increasing vigor to the Christian life of the faithful; to adapt more suitably to the needs of our own times those institutions which are subject to change; to foster whatever can promote union among all who believe in Christ; to strengthen whatever can help to call the whole of mankind into the household of the Church. The Council therefore sees particularly cogent reasons for undertaking the reform and promotion of the liturgy." Contained within the document were general principles on liturgical reforms that would bring sacramental life embodied in the Eucharist contextualized and inculturated within communities.

experiences and lives. For GenXers, it's about the freedom to establish meaning that is particularized and relevant, what the French anthropologist, Claude Lèvi Strauss, called "bricolage" or the putting together various pieces of symbols, teaching, tradition, and images for a particular context, experience, or situation.[7] Rodger Nishioka highlights the proclivity and value to form and reshape meaning as outcomes of being in a "liquid culture and a liquid church."[8] Nishioka describes the liquid church as one that "embraces ambiguity, mystery, wonder, and awe," a community that "lives easily and comfortably with paradox and irony and values ardor more than order."[9] Beaudoin sees that what might appear as a confused, ambiguous spiritual quest on the part of GenXers, is actually indicative of a deep spirituality that is in progress.[10]

This provides an opening for the Church in ministry today. The Church has been given "gifts of God for the people of God." In the Word—written, baked, fermented, and

---

[7] Virtual Faith: The Irreverent Spiritual Quest of Generation X by Tom Beaudoin (San Francisco: Jossey Bass, 1998), 149.

[8] "Life in the Liquid Church: Ministry in a Consumer Culture" by Rodger Nishioka in Journal for Preachers. no. 26.1 (Advent 2002), 31. Nishioka credited the originator of the concept "liquid church" to Dr. Pete Ward of King College, London, who drew the image from a book by Zygmunt Bauman, Liquid Modernity (Malden, MA: Blackwell Publishers, 2000).

[9] Nishioka, loc. cit., 34.

[10] Beaudoin, op. cit, 163-168. Also Mark Yaconelli's observation:

"Christian practices are the means through which Christians seek to respond to God's invitation of Love. They are the habits, disciplines, and patterns of life through which Christians seek communion with Christ and solidarity with others. Just as Paul invites the Ephesians to be imitators of God, Christian practices are the way in which Christians seek to imitate the intentions and patterns of Jesus Christ."

From Mark Yaconelli, "Focusing Youth Ministry through Christian Practices" in Starting Right: Thinking Theologically About Youth Ministry (Grand Rapids: Zondervan, 2000) by Kenda Creasy Dean, Chap Clark, Dave Rahn. Reprinted with permission.

hydrolyzed—we find the means by and through which God's Spirit nourishes, calls, and sends the community to the world. Reformed theology has held to the equal importance of both the preached and spoken Word (Scripture and sermon) and the sacraments, the former being the verbal witness to the life, death, and resurrection of Jesus Christ, and the latter being the physical embodiment of that testified reality. Word and Sacrament are like hand and glove.

But, I think, something is harmfully missing from this picture. What the 8am-ers and the GenXers teach us is that the community matters. Sacramental history has been dotted with efforts by the Church to explain the mystery of the Eucharist. GenXers live in a liquid culture in which precision is not the requirement, but living in the experience of the mystery is. Sacramentology treats us to the buffet of attempts at explaining the change of elements and substances:

- *transubstantiation* (changing of the substance from bread to the actual body of Christ, and wine to the actual blood of Christ),
- *consubstantiation* (the substance of Christ's body and blood is in, with, and under the elements of the bread and wine),
- *sacramental union* (as the bread and wine are ingested, the Spirit mysteriously unites the community to one another and to the glorified Christ in heaven),
- *transignification* (the bread as the "body of Christ" can signify Christ's crucified body, the Church as Christ's body on earth, Christ's glorified body, the bread on the table—all simultaneously), and
- *transelementation* (just as iron thrust into fire does not change the fact it is still iron, and fire is still fire, but that the iron's element is changed in some way, so, too, the

bread is changed by its sacramental union with Christ, but remains bread, just as Christ remains Christ).[11]

The deficiency of these efforts, sadly, has been to place the spotlight on the bread and the cup themselves, rather than on the action of the community and the community for which Christ died and rose. Theologians began with the premise that something must happen to the bread and wine in order for the benefits of Christ's work to have any operation and significance for people's lives, both now and eternally. Church councils were called and creeds, confessions, and a lot of theological inquiries were developed to devise a system of answers. What would begin to happen if, combined with the treasure of almost two millennia of learning and discourse, we looked for a Eucharistic theology from the community's act of celebrating our Lord's banquet? What would be unleashed if we looked to how the Spirit is at work in, with, under, above, and among the people of God and allow them to speak and teach each other, pastors, and professional theologians? What would the Spirit say through them/us?

Liturgical theology, GenXers, and the liquid church/liquid culture call the Church back to its roots. Like peeling the onion skins to get to the core, the Church finds its life in the authentic and real combined with the inherited tradition of the great cloud of witnesses. It is no longer a bifurcated dichotomy of sacred vs. profane, holy vs. unholy, churched vs. unchurched vs. overchurched. Rather, it's a retrieval of proclaiming that all are sacred, that God has called all things "good." Where do we find such a testimony? Yes, from the Word read and proclaimed. Yes, from the Word sealed—eaten,

---

[11] The Italian reformer, Peter Martyr Vermigli, retrieved this term from an image depicted earlier by the early church fathers, St. Gregory of Naziansus and Cyril of Alexandria. Discussed in "The Bread That We Break: Toward a Chalcedonian Resolution of the Eucharistic Controversies" Princeton Seminary Bulletin vol. 24, no. 2 (2003) by George Hunsinger.

drank/intincted, poured/dipped/sprinkled. And yes, from the community.

What does a sacramental community-in-action look like? How might a Eucharistic theology emerge and be expressed by the community to the glory of God? Let me suggest that a dynamic liturgical theology involves a **thinking, praying, fellowshipping,** and **talking** congregation/presbytery/General Assembly/one holy catholic apostolic Church, akin to the actions we find summarized in Acts 2:42. This means that at every level, we lift up:

Family Talk. Departing from the traditional stricture of the pastor or priest solely addressing the community with occasional responses from the pew, let's encourage conversation and dialogue, perhaps serving the Eucharist around mini-Tables, or if your congregation is small enough, have everyone sit around the Table. This is what we did at the Eucharistic meal my congregation celebrated during Maundy Thursday. There were less than 15 who showed up, so we placed four movable pews around the Table, ate and intincted around the Table, while laughing and talking. In Filipino culture, siblings are called *magkakapatid,* which means to be cut-off from the same intestine or *bituka*.[12] Because you need your intestine to digest food and absorb nutrients, food and dining have great significance for family life and family talk in Filipino homes. Table conversation enables the community to discover the organic unity within the gathered body of Christ with the glorified body of Christ.

Family Meals. The late Episcopalian liturgical scholar, Thomas Julian Talley (1924-2005), reportedly observed that the Table is not like any table in the world, but it is like any other

---

[12] For more on Filipino *intestinal theology,* see Ecumenical and Prophetic: The Witness of the United Church of Christ in the Philippines by Melanio La Guardia Aoanan (Quezon City, Philippines: Claretian Publications, 1998), 39-40.

table in the world.[13] When the Church gathered is the Church scattered, the Church does not cease being the Church. Whether congregants and clergy find themselves dining at home, at a local eatery, enjoying a scone and latté at a café, or sipping some Pinot Noir on a beach blanket with family and friends, we ought to challenge and encourage the Church to see that every table setting is a holy time and holy place given by God. Every enjoyment of food and drink becomes a eucharistic moment. It helps the Church to think theologically throughout the week, on any given day, prompting genuine offerings of thanks, and encouraging us to view the Eucharistic meal celebrated on the Lord's Day as deeply connected to every occasion for table fellowship and vice versa.

Family Plus. We become part of the household of God at our baptism, a covenantal vow that is renewed by the baptized individual and the community again and again as the baptismal vows are lived and nurtured. Theologian Leanne van Dyke has called it "baptismal living."[14] In a 1998 article, "Indiscriminate Baptism and Baptismal Integrity," preaching and worship scholar Ronald Byars argued that the most critical liturgical issue facing the Presbyterian Church (U.S.A.) is how seriously the baptized community takes our baptismal commitments. We need to call our congregations back to what it means to be brothers and sisters in the household of God; this begins at baptism, and continues throughout life, interdependently linked to the Table. This means engaging the whole congregation, laity and clergy alike, in learning the richness of the Church's sacramentology. Here I mean not just our Reformed

---

[13] Anecdote shared in Eucharist doctoral seminar, Spring 2006, Drew University, by the Rev. Dr. James Farwell, the late Dr. Talley's colleague at the General Theological Seminary in New York City, who taught liturgics there.

[14] Core Cluster meeting of the Re-Forming Ministry Initiative of the Office of Theology and Worship, Presbyterian Church (U.S.A.) in June 2005, Western Theological Seminary, Holland, MI, where the Core Cluster gathered to consider how baptism exhibits the one holy catholic apostolic Church.

sacramentology, but also lessons that we can learn from the one holy catholic apostolic Church—East, West, North, and South. As I have argued in this chapter, learning is not merely book learning. There certainly has to be plenty of assiduous study on our congregations' part to comb the treasures of the Church's sacramentology. But, more importantly, how do we begin to think and live theologically with integrity so that what we do and what we believe shape and inform each other?

Perhaps, through the process of family talk, family meal, and living out what it means to be in the family, the Spirit of God will help us to discover with renewed freshness and vitality who we really are and whose we really are.

But a word of caution. Just as easily as we bandy about the term and concept "family" to describe and prescribe what the Church is and ought to be, we can become complacently content with the sense of family when we believe that we have all the characteristics of what it means to be "family of God." While the sacraments of baptism and the Eucharist and theological engagement with those sacraments will effect and enrich the reality of family in the Church, the sacraments testify to a still deeper and lasting reality: the kingdom of God.

In a postmodern time, family infuses church life and witness with the sense of belongingness and identity—twin hungers of everyone inside and outside the Church. But, the reality of "kingdom of God" deepens belongingness and identity by calling the Church and the world to the Christ who is both in and with us (family) and who transcends our time and space (kingdom).

Isn't that what John the Baptist's preparation, Jesus' own preaching and story-telling, and the Church's own apostolic witness all point to—the presence of the kingdom of God already but still to come? It's the duality of the kingdom's here-but-not-yet reality that is a healthy and real reminder that we belong to one another as we belong to God. We wouldn't get that, necessarily, with the "family" concept because family fails us from time to time (that's why we have unchurched and overchurched people). By placing "kingdom of God" side-by-side with the reality of "family," as the sacraments themselves do, we come to discover that the God who rules the world, the Church, and our hearts transforms all the imperfections and dysfunction of "family" and creates and re-creates something marvelous; and it's this transformative aspect of God's work through the family that helps us to see that we are being called to the real reality of all the stuff that we do (and don't do) as the Church. This happens, precisely, because the kingdom of God has come and is still to come.

Response by Laura S. Mendenhall
to Neal D. Presa on Sacraments

Neal D. Presa's work with "Stale Bread & Sour Wine: Keeping the Gospel Real through the Sacraments" names the issues. Clearly this congregation's experience of the Gospel becomes real to them as they share the bread and the cup with one another. In the stories Neal tells, members of the congregation are real with one another and with him during their participation with one another in the Lord's Supper. Such stories lead me to believe that in these moments members of the congregation are also real with God as God's presence becomes real to them. Neal's stories of his congregation are a graphic description of the Body of Christ, not just as the bread is broken but also as the church becomes the Body of Christ broken for one another and for this hurting world.

For me one of the most touching parts of Neal's story is that the congregation teaches him how to be their pastor, teaches him how to keep the Gospel real through the sacraments. It is only in this openness to learning that a pastor can continue to be alive to the Gospel and grow in service to Christ. If a seminary graduate thinks he/she has already learned all that is needed in order to serve Christ's church, if he/she ever thinks that the only way to continue to be educated for ministry is through another course taken or another book read, then this person is not ready to serve as a pastor. Few debate that a congregation needs a pastor. Congregations need a Biblically and theologically trained pastor who will read and interpret Scripture with them, who will help them discern God's calling to them and where God is sending them, who will accompany them to a cemetery proclaiming, "In life and in death we belong to God." However, while a congregation needs the depth of a pastor's study, the pastor needs the depth of a congregation's knowing. This is part of the sacred dance of a congregation and a pastor, celebrating the way God calls us into a partnership in Christ's reign *on earth as it is in heaven.*

Neal Presa is a pastor who is dancing with his congregation as they worship God together. In their worship both this congregation and this pastor are being shaped for ministry—*lex orandi, lex credendi.* In this context I would like to pose some questions, wanting not to disturb any of the rich sacramental work this congregation is doing but simply to explore what might be the next step in the dance.

Neal does a wonderful job of describing the situation of a forty member congregation that is caught in a "battle between the 8am-ers vs. the 10:30am-ers vs. the unifiers." Much of Neal's description is of the 8am service and the very rich experience of God's presence through the sacrament of the Lord's Supper. Their weekly celebration of the Eucharist has formed them into a tight cohesive communion with one another. They are family for each other. Apparently, their commitment to their particular way of worshipping, to their favorite hymns, and to one another has kept them from worshipping with the 10:30am-ers. Is there any chance they have fallen into the trap of worshipping their own worship? Could their experience of the Table be enriched further by the addition at the Table of the 11am-ers or newcomers? Can the Gospel continue to be real for a part of the Body of Christ that is segregating itself from the rest of the Body, particularly the nearest part of the Body, the other 30 members of the church? Is part of the reality of the Gospel missing when part of the Body is missing? Neal does not mention whether or not new members are joining the church. If they are, which service do new members attend? I'm led to believe newcomers would be attending the 10:30 a.m. service. If the 8am-ers are as "cutting edge, not fearing to learn and certainly not fearing to teach" as Neal describes, I would challenge them to open themselves to both learning from and teaching the 10:30am-ers what they know about the reality of the Gospel through their experience of the sacrament.

I can imagine that the Generation X-ers, who presumably are at the 10:30 a.m. service, might be eager for this very real experience of God's presence that the 8am-ers know. GenXers long for a deep connection with the reality of the Gospel. GenXers know that community matters. GenXers know what it means for the Body of Christ, the church, to be broken and poured out for the sake of the world. Isn't there a lot that the 8am-ers and the 10:30am-ers have to teach one another, a lot they have to learn from one another? I encourage Neal, as pastor, to celebrate what each part of his congregation understands about the reality of the Gospel and, just as the 8am-ers have taught him, find a way for the 8am-ers to teach the 10:30 am-ers and vice versa. I can imagine that such an opening up to one another as the Body of Christ might open up the whole family to welcoming to the Table "the blind, the outcasts, the hemorrhaging woman, the merchants," as Neal described them. Perhaps this would be such a "leap" experience that Neal described as Pentecostal.

Neal has given us a profound pastoral truth: "all are sacred." All are part of the Body of Christ, broken and poured out for one another and for this hurting world. This is the Gospel reality we know through the sacraments. Out of his own strong sacramental theology and his own compassionate pastor's heart, out of what he has learned from the 8am-ers, I invite Neal to encourage the 8am-ers and the 10:30am-ers to be the Body of Christ for one another and for those beyond their walls. Bring them to the Table together and allow them to place in one another's hands the Bread of Life and the Cup of Salvation. In this way the Body of Christ makes a bold statement about the reality of the Gospel for all God's family.

One of the things I miss most, having left the congregation to serve in a seminary, is the full experience of being the Body of Christ together and for one another—young and old, long-time members and newcomers, folks from a variety of backgrounds and traditions and theological standings. The congregation I most recently served provided a nursery for visitors who were uncomfortable bringing their children into the sanctuary, but all ages worshipped together. It could get messy, but we recognized the importance of having each one present, to learn from one each one the reality of the Gospel through the sacraments. We knew that without the babies receiving the waters of baptism, we would forget that it is not because of our study of Scripture or our confession of faith that Christ loves us, but only out of God's grace. Without the children wiggling their way through worship and dropping the bread crumbs, we would forget the need to say clearly what we believe, would forget that not everything we believe about the mystery of God can be put into words. Without the continual nudging from teenagers, we would skip over the big difficult questions. Without adults who face life's realities, who would carry the load for the Gospel's reality? Without older adults to set the Table, who would teach us Table manners? Without those who read Scripture differently, how will we be open to setting aside our own knowing that we might hear the fullness of God's Word? Without those who are baptismal brothers and sisters being willing to place in our hands the bread of life and the cup of salvation, how will we be fed? Thanks be to God for the Body of Christ that keeps the Gospel real through the sacraments.

VIII

Community

Elizabeth "Liz" Kaznak

All who believed were together and had all things in common; they would sell their possessions and goods and distribute the proceeds to all, as any had need. Day by day, as they spent much time together in the temple, they broke bread at home and ate their food with glad and generous hearts, praising God and having the goodwill of all the people. And day by day the Lord added to their number those who were being saved.

Acts 2:44-47

We live in a remarkable and challenging time in history. Never before have human beings had such instant access to people, cultures, religions, and information and yet research consistently reports people feel more lonely and disconnected than ever before. There are many aspects of modern life that we can point to as contributors to this reality: families separated, mobility of people, individualism, technology, etc. All of these factors can make it more difficult to hold communities of people meaningfully together. The other side of challenge as we know it, however, is opportunity. What we have realized through these newfound challenges is even though community life is more challenging to create and sustain, the longing for community has not diminished.

People need people. We need each other to care about and be cared for. We need each other for support and enrichment. We desire to be connected to a group of people that share in common something larger than themselves, and we need rituals and practices that shape and form us in our life

102

together as we strive to embrace our calling as children of God. It's as old as creation and as sure as God's grace; we are meant to live life in community. We do not know ourselves outside of our relationships with other people. We need one another to understand ourselves as well as to thrive. To paraphrase Reinhold Niebuhr, a prominent theologian, we know ourselves in relationship to the other. Our Christian faith is built on the foundation of God's love, peace and justice lived in community. And we have the story, rituals and practices to shape and form our becoming as the living Body of Christ in the world.

The church where I serve is in an area of the city where lots of young people gather at all times of the day in coffee houses and bars. It appears as though community life is thriving. Five years ago we were just starting a new church and wondered what some of the folks who were regulars in these establishments were looking for in their lives. So we did our own research. Nothing fancy or highly technical. We just took a camera and some key questions and hit the streets looking for individuals willing to talk to us. Over and over again we heard the same response: I am looking for community. I want to belong to a group of people that accept me for who I am, but challenge me to grow. We began to explore what that might mean. As pastors engaged in ministry in the church in the world, we were particularly interested in bridging the gap, or at least potentially being a bridge over the gap, for people seeking community and God but not necessarily seeking God within the communities in which they were participating. It was our conviction that the way of Christ, which gave birth to the early church community held some of the key elements to meaningful community life. One of Jesus' first responses to his baptism in the gospels is the call of the disciples to come and follow. Jesus does not strike out alone, but invites a community to travel that road with him. In the early church, Paul reflects in his letters that the church is the body of Christ. They are the community of people that will embody the message and ministry of Christ and live it out in community and in the world. The early Christians understood that their faith gave them a distinctive identity, an identity shared with other Christians by virtue of their faith and practices, which would shape them as the living Body of Christ, born of the same Spirit. (John 3:8)

This identity created a unity and commitment that transcended family ties (or simply expanded them) to the degree that they lived for the good of the whole and not for the self alone. In other words, individualism was not an aspect of community life. Rather, community life in Christ was lived as depicted in Acts 2 where the community formed its identity in Christ and lived his message of devotion to God, self-giving, forgiveness and support for the needs of the marginalized and oppressed. By caring for one another in this way, the life of faith is more fully realized through practice.

The kind of community life Paul points to has a common identity that not only holds it together, but allows that community to transcend space and time. Life in Christ as the living body connects us with all who have come before, those who worship in other lands, in other ways and in our own congregations. "Now you are the body of Christ and individually members of it." (1 Corinthians 12:27) This is the eternal and transcendent nature of the church. Just as there is this universal connection, there is the need for a local or individual expression of that community life to be lived.

When we gather for worship as a congregation we live an expression of that greater body in the way we worship, care for one another and serve those in need in our communities. This movement of the life of the living body appealed to us as we were looking at how to be more intentional about living the message of Christ. The elements that seemed to give shape to the Christian community included an Inward Journey, a Communal Journey and an Outward Journey. So we devised a church model that would facilitate the Inward, Outward and Communal Journey within the arms of small intentional communities. Each of these elements, when present and balanced, gives meaning, direction and purpose to the community.

> *We believe God calls each of us to a life of love and service. To paraphrase Frederick Buechner, "God calls us to the place where our deep gladness and the world's deep hunger meet." This calling is lived out when we join our passions and gifts with God's work of creating Shalom—a world of peace, justice and celebration. We believe that through Intentional Communities we can most effectively discern our calls, be equipped to live them out and experience Shalom in our own lives.*
> *- from the Intentional Community Handbook*

The Outward Journey: Co-Creating God's Shalom

After five years of working with the Intentional Communities we have discovered that the Outward Journey is the most central element to the ongoing success and vitality of an Intentional Community. When we first began Covenant Community Church, we made a commitment to only start intentional communities around a shared outward call. When that outward call was completed or was no longer the central element to the group, we would encourage its participants to end the group and bless and send the members to some other outward mission.

We explored the "cell group" model that starts groups around a trained leader for the purpose of growing the group and then splitting to start new groups. If we would have used this model we probably would be three to five times larger in numbers. Another option available was the "support group" model in which groups are formed around a shared existential issue like drug abuse, healthy eating, or raising children. Or we could have used an "affinity group" model, which starts groups based on social affinity and personal interests (men's groups, age groups, singles, Bible studies, prayer groups). But we didn't.

We decided that to be a church (Intentional Community), we must first have a shared outward calling and make that calling the central purpose and focus of the community. The central characteristic of an Intentional Community is to participate in the ongoing creation of God's Shalom (peace, justice, wholeness and celebration) in the world by following the way of Christ. We believe this Shalom happens through all three elements of our communities (In, With, Out), but for a community to start it must first have a defined outward calling. When some other element becomes central to the life of the group, whether it be spiritual practices, community life, friendships, or personal support, it becomes less than an intentional community. The community may still be important to its members, but it is not fully an intentional community. We have learned that when a group forgets its shared Outward Journey or the outward mission becomes secondary to any of the other elements the group is headed down a path to dissolution. When a group's outward vision is no longer able to evoke the commitment, it's too small, members in the community will turn toward nit picking or just stop coming altogether. When this process begins the community will need either to rethink and reclaim its original vision or dissolve and encourage members to discern a new calling and create a new community. This commitment to the centrality of the Outward Journey may be one of our most important decisions and possibly the key to our community's transformative power.

The Inward Journey

The Inward Journey focuses on an intentional journey into the life of God and into the transcendent space that flows in and through the community. This journey often happens best through forms of meditation, contemplation and reflection.

Many groups have experimented with *Lectio Divina*, Guided Imagery, Guided Meditation, Yoga, and Centering Prayer. Other practices can include Bible Study and Shared Reading. Inward practices help us dissolve the boundaries between self, God and (other) and so expand possibilities of relationship. A good discerning question when trying to decide if the practice is an inward or communal practice (the two are often confused) is to ask, "Does this practice invite me to open myself up to an experience of God or is this practice a discussion 'about' God?" A good and effective inward practice is one that invites us into a full body, mind and soul experience of God's presence! An inward practice helps us to experience God not just think about God! Good spiritual practices may include "thinking" but they do not stop there.

The Inward Journey focuses our attention not necessarily on each other (communal) and not necessarily on the needs of the world (outward), but specifically on the Divine that connects and holds everything together. This journey often has an individual focus, because it is the consciousness of the individual that is needing to be evoked and expanded. However, these individually focused practices should be done in community. There is a heightened energy and awareness that happens when we do inward practices in community. The energy of the Inward Journey is one of openness and expansiveness even though the focus seems inward and particular.

The Communal Journey

The final circle in the Intentional Community Model is, "With." "With" is how we are in relating to and supporting one another. We have said that an Intentional Community is a group of people who covenant to gather on a regular basis for the purpose of participating in God's shalom (peace, justice, wholeness and celebration) by following the way of Christ with

107

their lives. In Genesis we learn that it is not good for us to be alone. We are made to be in relationship with one another, indeed, with all of creation. Being together as the body of Christ in small groups is one of the ways we practice what we believe. How can we truly know what it means to be forgiven and to reconcile with another, if we do not have opportunities to practice this in community? How can we take care of each other, bear one another's burdens, if we do not know each other well enough to be of aid? Being together intentionally in small groups gives us a realistic opportunity to be present to each other in ways that are relevant to our lives. The tension of course in a small group is to balance the needs of any individual with the needs of the group as a whole. The whole is greater than the individual parts, yet the parts, each individual, are important.

The design of our time together as an intentional community is to facilitate the tension of paying attention to the individual as well as the health of the group. At the start of each meeting each person should have a chance to share with the people in their groups something that is currently happening in their lives. The check-in time is not intended to be a history of the week, or an invitation into therapy, but a time simply to share the most pressing or joyful moments of the week. In intentionally making time to know one another and what is happening in our lives we are better able to support and nurture each other.

When a group is newly forming the check-in, communal time will take a much larger share of the meeting than normal. Group dynamics tells us that when a group is forming, bonding, getting to know each other, is the most important thing we do. As the group becomes more familiar, usually by the sixth meeting, the time spent should be more evenly dispersed between the three elements. Again, when a group or a person is ending their relationship with an intentional community, we need to spend time honoring each other and the experience of being in community so we can end well.

The person serving in the role of Care Coordinator (CC) is in charge of the check-in time. This seems easy, but in addition to asking the opening question for check-in he or she should be paying particular attention to the group dynamics. It is the job of the Care Coordinator to nurture the health of the group. The CC should be mindful of any one person dominating group discussion, as well as the person who is not speaking up at all. The CC should pay attention to the overall health of the community and how it is taking care of its members. Sometimes the CC is the person who coordinates efforts like meals or cards when needed, but that responsibility can be shared. Finally, the CC is in charge of debriefing the meeting. Debriefing is a time when we reflect on what was particularly helpful or unhelpful in our time together. Debriefing is not a time for new business or ganging up on someone but to help us air any grievances in the spirit if love and forgiveness so we can meet again as Christ's reconciled community.

Being in community is wonderful and challenging. Communities go through so many transitions in their life together. Yet we all know that life without community would be terribly empty. Paul's words to the church in Colossians breathe true: *Clothe yourselves with kindness, gentleness, meekness and compassion. But most of all clothe yourselves with love, which binds everything together in perfect harmony. And be thankful.* (Colossians 3:12-15, author's paraphrase) Community life is intended to be a reflection of the grace, peace, love and justice of God. This is made possible when we live together, intentionally grounded in that love.

References
Holy Bible, New Revised Standard Version (Coksebury, 1989)
Dietrich Bonhoeffer, *Life Together* (San Francisco: Harper, 1954)

Response by John T. Galloway, Jr.
to Liz Kaznak on Community

A major advantage to structuring this book in a dialogue fashion is that we get to articulate the diverse perspectives from which we live out God's word. Liz Kaznak and I complement each other on the subject of community. I put my stress on the <u>initiating</u> work of God through the Holy Spirit. She gives us guidance on how best to <u>respond</u>. Both perspectives are needed.

I want to underscore all that Liz has written and add to it explicit language that I believe is implicit in her fine essay. Acts 2 is about the Holy Spirit coming upon the disciples, empowering them to be the Church. So I want to inject Holy Spirit language. The text Liz has chosen is one of my favorites. Acts 2:44-47 describes what happens to a group when the Holy Spirit moves within and among.

The Outward Journey as Liz terms it is what Jesus predicted in Acts 1:8, "But you will receive power when the Holy Spirit has come upon you; and you will be my witnesses in Jerusalem, in all Judea and Samaria, and to the ends of the earth." We get our word "dynamite" from the Greek term translated "power." Jesus is suggesting that God's Shalom comes not from comfortable discussions of current events or as our consciences are eased by comforting words that are little more than a religious sedative. God's Shalom comes as the Spirit explodes within a fellowship that is ready to face the ugly reality of human need in our world. Liz has put well the importance of "focus" as the Spirit acts through us on specific matters. I personally find it disturbing that the church today has too often lost both its social focus and spiritual power in the public square. On this score I found Liz's words refreshing.

The Inward Journey. Here Liz takes us from acting together in work for social justice to our personal need for the Lord in our lives: in the language of a former generation—collective social action to more individual personal piety within the group.

A fascinating topic for some future sermon would be to juxtapose the words "All" and "Each" in the early verses of Acts 2. "… All together in one place … All were filled." "… A tongue rested on each of them." The Pentecost experience was both communal and individual. Perhaps this is why, in our worship, we pray the communal prayer saying together, "Our Father…" and together we each confess our individual faith, "I believe… ." For all the collective aspects of Acts 2 there is also very much that Inward Journey Liz writes about.

When I read her important question, "Does this practice invite me to open myself up to an experience of God or is this practice a discussion 'about' God," two homiletical brain cells twitched in my memory bank.

The first reminded me of the dramatic audience change that occurs in verses 4 and 5 of the 23rd Psalm. I have found it helpful at funerals to remind the congregation that the psalmist begins, "The Lord." (I'm talking about God here. You, congregation, are my audience as we ponder stuff about God. God makes me lie down in green pastures; God leads me … God restores.) But then, when the psalmist begins to reflect on that time in the valley of the shadow of death, the congregation is forgotten. It is suddenly a personal devotional moment. The psalmist is awestruck, moved, turned. God is the audience. God is being experienced. "… You are with me; your rod and your staff—they comfort me. You prepare … you anoint … ." With verse 6 the psalmist seems to come out of it and goes back to addressing the congregation. In the midst of talking "about" God, the psalmist has a powerful experience "of" God.

The other brain cell in my memory bank carried recollection of Barbara Brown Taylor's wisdom about how

111

people in our churches are constantly clamoring for more "Bible Study." Haven't we heard that? She tried to give her congregants what they said they wanted. She gave them "Bible Studies," and the response was the same old same old. Then one day she realized that "Bible Study" was a code phrase meaning "I want to experience God." She began to use so called "Bible Studies" as an opportunity for helping people experience God on the Inward Journey and wonderful things began to happen.

Thank you, Liz, for verbalizing such an important question: "Does this practice invite me to open myself up to an experience of God, or is this practice a discussion 'about' God?"

Outward Journey. Inward Journey. Communal Journey

Perhaps no mark of the Holy Spirit was more salient than the new Communal Journey it prompted. The world was stunned at what it saw. These early Christians treated each other in a revolutionary way. These Christians cared for each other, carried each other, supported each other. One of the most powerful witnesses of the early church was in how folks treated each other, perhaps a reminder to us whose members don't always treat each other very well.

As Liz and I pool our language the reader might wonder is this "intentional community" our intention or the Lord's intention and the answer is "Yes." Community is a pooling of intention. "We love because he first loved us." (1 John 4:19) We proclaim a theology that declares God's starting of the matter. God's grace was given to me almost 2000 years before I was born. My life is a response to what God has done and an openness to what God by the Holy Spirit can do in and through me. It is about God. This needs to be emphasized.

But so does our response. Liz has taken on the difficult task of working from Acts 2 to offer guidance on how to shape our response.

I call it a difficult task because when the Holy Spirit comes upon a person or a fellowship, instruction is needed on how to respond and alas is all too often ignored or rejected. Persons filled with the Spirit too often refuse to listen to anyone because they claim they are getting all the cues they need directly from the Lord. Discipline and order and genuine community suffer. Legitimate ecclesiastical authority is lost.

Some readers who are at home in what we call the "charismatic renewal" might see no problem with shunning any authority other than our own personal pipeline to God. You might wonder why, if I have the Spirit in my life, do I need any discipline or instruction or correction from someone who has ecclesiastical authority when I don't even know if the person "has the Spirit." The argument is heartfelt and offered with determination. But the argument would carry more weight if the Spirit filled person's criterion for judging whether the authority figure has the Spirit or not didn't so often rest on whether said authority happens to agree with the Spirit filled person's opinions or not. Let's remember that if Spirit filled fellowships didn't need major instruction from outside, Paul would not have needed to write to the Corinthians. And of course, if Spirit filled fellowships readily accepted such instruction Paul would not have needed to write them again and again and again.

As we respond to what God has done in Jesus Christ and as we are open to how the Holy Spirit moves within and among us, we all need to take a regular dose of First and Second Corinthians, especially 1 Corinthians 11-14 and the teachings about the Body of Christ. Our response to God's initiative needs guidance. And yes a reread of Liz Kaznak's chapter will help as well.

IX

Decently and In Good Order:
Resolving Conflicts
When People Do Not Want To

Bruce Reyes-Chow

The year was 1999 and I was about to enter the final worship service at my first call. Right out of seminary, I received a plum call in San Francisco as a solo pastor in a multicultural Redevelopment/New Church Development. The previous four years in that ministry had been, at times, wonderfully supportive, freeing and joyful. It had also been four years of ministry fraught with anguish, frustration and an overall conflicted situation that neither the congregation nor I handled well.

Without boring you with too many of the whiny details, my four years went something like this ... all from my perspective, of course:

▸ I am 26, right out of seminary and while I know how to pretend to listen to folks, I *really* do think I know it all.
▸ No one likes my ideas—clearly there is something wrong with them. No one loves or appreciates me.
▸ Ministry sucks.
▸ I Quit.

While I do know that all the conflict was not my fault, I often reflect on what I could have done differently in order that everyone would have had a better experience. I don't think it was *purely* my age or lack of experience that led to the conflicted situation, but rather the approach that many in the congregation and I took towards the conflict. Rather than see conflict as something that could help us move forward as a community, we saw it as something to be conquered, hidden or ignored. And while any or all of those approaches worked or felt good for short periods of time, these were not productive or fruitful long-term solutions for dealing with conflict in that congregation, or anywhere else for that matter.

I fear that this is not an isolated experience or feeling for many first-call pastors, especially in urban settings. Heck, I am sure that many seasoned folks still see conflict as something to be avoided at all costs. After being away from that situation for about six years and working with other congregations in different capacities around conflict, I have noticed that most conflict management is not really about the end result or decision but about the process and journey that the community experiences. Central to this understanding of conflict management is to start, not with the nuts and bolts process, but by shifting our entire approach and perception of conflict itself.

I wish that there were a list of ten things that would guarantee conflict well resolved and managed but like most things in life, there are not. Rather than offer any "tools" or quick "fixes" for ministry, which hinge upon our own particular gifts, I can offer some "musings" on conflict that I hope will be added and adapted to the approaches and perspectives of others to this blessing and struggle that we call conflict.

Conflict as Reality

I am not sure if it is cultural DNA (my Asian American-ness, which would rather avoid than confront), or just what I have been taught through my church experience, but I came into ministry with this crazy notion that I was above conflict. We don't really have to fight, do we? Can't we all just gather in the name of Christ, hold hands, sing Kum Ba Ya and just get along? I still remember a conversation during my first week on the job when someone who clearly needed to leave the church due to previous relationships wanted to remain there. If I were on the outside looking in and overhearing my response to this person, I would have thought, "What the #$^&* are you thinking?" But no, I said, "Sure, you can stay." With my mind really believing that I could be above the conflict, I set myself up for years of frustration.

Now I am in no way saying that we now adopt a posture of cynicism and paranoia when it comes to ministry. I would posit rather that we take the approach that conflict is natural and not always negative. Our posture should be to see conflict as a natural part of living in human community that we need to acknowledge and handle accordingly instead of as something to run from. Conflict will surely occur at different levels and intensities, but if we see conflict as something to be managed and navigated rather than avoided or conquered we will all have a better chance of thriving in ministry.

Conflict as Contextual

And while conflict is a natural part of any community, it will play itself out in different ways depending on the context. Taking into account cultural and personal differences is crucial if we are to shift to a healthier approach to conflict. Here are a few examples of how conflict may manifest itself:

Generational Conflict. Let me over-generalize as I am prone to do: when it comes to sticking it out in the face of tough times, my generation is pretty bad. Too often we run at the first sign of struggle and fail to work through the tough parts of being in relationship or community. Now in no way am I saying that all the blame is to be laid on those born after 1964, the GenXers. We learned this approach to life from our parents, the Boomers who in turn adopted it by rebelling against their

116

parents, that Silent Generation. No longer were the boomers going to stay in a job or a relationship, at all costs. Advances in technology and globalization have only sped that process up for us. The struggle for us now is to be able to discern when conflict really is too intense instead of acting on our first impulse to run far away. We need to be more measured in our response to conflict. Is the conflict *really* to the point where there can be no reconciliation? If there is only possibility for continued emotional, physical or spiritual abuse, it is critical to get out, but if it is a matter of holding difficult conversations that can lead to transformation and healing, we need to be willing to stay in the midst of the conflict long enough to see the other side.

Cultural Conflict. How does one deal with conflict when cultural norms often create different rules? Dealing well with cultural context is one of the lost arts of conflict management, particularly in the case of ethnicity. One of the things we have been taught in Western culture is not to "Triangulate" in relationships. When this term was first explained to me, I thought to myself, "Uh oh, now my family will never be able to communicate." In my Asian American context, I have counted on triangulation to deliver my point to the right people, and I counted on triangulation to hear the voices and perspectives of others. Now I come to find out that it is wrong?

In many Asian American communities, triangulation is the main vehicle for sharing information and dealing with conflict, not to mention day-to-day activities of the family. There is comfort in knowing that you can share a gripe with one member of the family and it will be carried to the other. In this way, everyone "saves face," the conflict is identified and more times than not, reconciled. Now of course, there are many ways this can go wrong, but in the Asian American context, if one does not understand this dynamic, ministry can go terribly wrong. How many times have we heard about non-Asians serving Asian American congregations and placing Western styles of conflict resolution upon the community? Or what about

117

the Asian American pastor who goes to a predominately White congregation and is bulldozed by the overly confrontational Western mode of conflict resolution? Both situations have happened to far too many friends and congregations to be ignored. If we hope to mange conflict well, we must understand that there are cultural intricacies that when brought into our approach will help a community thrive.

There are also many variables within evaluating context itself, including the following:

Gender. I have not thought a great deal about this, but instinctually, I know that men and women tend to handle conflict differently. I am not always able to put a finger on it, but as I sit in meetings, mediate conversations and counsel couples, I notice differences. Now we can argue whether it is nature or nurture that creates these differences, but the ways in which gender plays out in conflicts can, if we are not careful, be a forgotten variable. Since I am not foolish enough to speak for my female colleagues, I will only critique the boys. From my experience, it seems that despite our best intentions, we men still have an innate need to "mark" territory, to let folks know where they are in relationship to us. We seem to do this in all aspects of life, be it church, family, or work. This needs to claim our territory and space plays havoc on conflict management, which requires compromise and shifting. I am not sure where this comes from, but it seems like the male psyche perceives as weak giving any kind of ground in a conflicted situation. I am sure that it must have something to do with issues related to conquering land and peoples, or not wanting to give up the slain wooly mammoth for fear of starving, but whatever the reason or impetus, it is real and comes into play far too often in times of conflict.

Personality. Probably the biggest variable when it comes to evaluating conflict is that of individual personalities. It may seem relatively easy to talk in generalizations regarding generations, ethnicity and gender, but when one starts to put all these together with different life experiences and God-given personality traits, one can easily wonder how it is that any of us *ever* gets through conflicted situations with any sense of joy or hope. Yet personality does play a significant role in how we create, deal with and or mange conflict. As a pastor I have learned that being aware of the interaction between my own personality and these other contexts has helped me to see the particulars of others. Tools such as the Myers-Briggs and the Enneagram have proven invaluable to my own personal transformation as well as my ability to manage conflict within a congregation. Personality is perhaps the most ambiguous variable, one that calls upon our pastoral ability to assess individuals and communities and act appropriately.

Conflict as Compass

Okay, so here is the meat of the matter. This whole idea of shifting our approach to conflict does not do a darn bit of good if it doesn't affect how we lead, pastor and influence the churches we serve. We must be able to manage conflict in a way that moves the congregation forward.

I am a firm believer in the idea that if there is *no* conflict in a church, there is either some serious denial happening or the church is dead—not figuratively or metaphorically—but literally dead! I say this because, as I argued before, conflict is a natural part of being in community and human relationships. The artistry of ministry comes into play by developing the discipline to lead people through conflict in a way that moves a congregation through it into transformation.

While my "successes" have been few and far between, here are some approaches that might be helpful as we further hone our conflict management skills.

Be intentionally conversational. Too often we try to get rid of the conflict by moving too quickly towards resolution or decision-making. We set ourselves up for continued tensions by creating settings that feel either like debates or thinly veiled attempts to convince the other that they are wrong. I have found that most folks simply need to be heard in a way in which they know they will be taken seriously. Most folks don't even need to know that all their ideas and position will be adopted, but that they have been valued as a member of the community.

Be strategically quiet. Silence is painful sometimes. Too often pastors want to fill the uncomfortable void by saying something "profound." Now I am sure that much profundity does come forth out of silence, but sometimes we are called just to let things be. Ours is a culture of chaos, and sometimes we feel the need to create it even where there is none. I think that we pastors are often so well trained to thrive in chaos that we create it just so we have a place to shine. We want to speed things up so that we can achieve something measurable. Sometimes conflict just needs to *be* for a bit, given time to ruminate within people, so that the Spirit can do something with it that at the right time might be shared as a process of transformation and healing.

Be painfully transparent. Now, of course, there are boundaries that we must all stay within when it comes to our church relationships, but folks today are looking for authenticity and transparency when it comes to any situation in which they have invested some energy. This generation smells insincerity and hidden agendas like none other, so when it comes to handling conflict today, an atmosphere of openness must be created and nurtured. This applies to every aspect of our approach, from admitting when things are not going well to being open and honest about struggles. Basically, we must be open to what God has created us to be, nothing more, nothing less, always trying to grow into what God has intended for each of us. If we can bring that posture to the table, we will bring the kind of appropriate openness that will build the trust that is needed as we challenge and nurture folks through times of conflict.

In the end, when it gets right down to it, we can either decide that conflict is helpful or it is not. Once we each make that decision, the strategies and processes begin to take shape. I hope that I have made the case that conflict can be helpful when navigated with a posture of hope and authenticity. As we remember that God's transformation so often can come out of times of struggle, it is my hope that we may all be better equipped to pastor folks through the journey of conflict into the reality of transformation.

Response by Craig Barnes
to Bruce Reyes-Chow on Conflict

I always wince when I hear young pastors describe how they learned about conflict in the parish. That's because I know that there is only one way to do it, and it really hurts. There is also only one place to do it, and it's not in a seminary classroom. And I take a stab at lecturing on conflict in our seminary, but it is hard to inform a crisis that someone is going to have. You really have to be in the soup before you're ready to hear about survival plans. Bruce has provided a very good illustration of how quickly a pastor learns about conflict once the soup gets hot. And it always does.

It helps a great deal when pastors figure out, as Bruce did, that it is time to get over the "crazy notion" that we are "above conflict." We had better not be above it. Our calling is to lead the congregation by standing in the midst of the conflicts. Sometimes we even lead by causing the conflicts—as Jesus Christ demonstrated repeatedly. It isn't the fun part of the job, but there are times when it is the redemptive part.

Only the dead live without conflict. So yeah, I agree with Bruce. Conflict is a reality. It's a "natural part of living in human community," as he claims. But that is not because we all have strong opinions. It has taken me a while to figure this out, but the real source of conflict within any human community is the conflicted souls of those who are a part of it. Everything that grows experiences internal conflicts between what it was and what is now has to become. And it cannot become the new creation without necessarily losing something of the old one. That is "a natural part" of biological development, emotional maturity, and certainly our spiritual growth into Christians. But just because it is natural, that doesn't make it easy.

Even necessary losses can be resisted, and usually are. I have found that people prefer to express their conflicted feelings about their own lives by taking it out on the communities of which they are part—especially the church community since that is their best chance at shaking their fists toward God. No one really cares that much about the worship bulletin, flowers, flag, music or even the pastor. But they care more than they can express about the daughter who is getting married and moving away, the pending retirement, or the spouse who has a terrible disease. This means that it's the pastor's job to peer beneath the familiar debates about these things that really don't matter to find the spiritual sub-text that is always at work beneath the surface.

For example, the father who comes to see the pastor because he is upset that the youth director is taking the high school kids on a work-trip to the Dominican Republic isn't just concerned that it isn't safe, even though that is what he claims this conflict is about. He wouldn't be happy if a brigade of Marines went along. That's because his real concern is that his child is about to leave home, but he doesn't know how to prevent that. So, like the rest of us, he tries to control what he can. But it doesn't matter how many youth directors the pastor fires, this man is still going to lose his child. That is the real conflict and the real reason he needs a pastor.

While I appreciated Bruce's clear and helpful principles for "managing" conflict in a congregation, I was looking for insights that would distinguish him as a pastor. These management insights are extremely important and necessary to the survival of anyone who serves in leadership of a church. And I particularly appreciated his convincing caution that the principles of conflict management have to be shaped by cultural context. But at some point the pastor has to move beyond managing the presenting issues in a congregation to address the deeper issues of loss that usually fuel the congregational debates.

Just as it is necessary for pastors to look beneath the conflicts in their congregations, so it is critical that we look above the issue to ask, "What is God's conflict with this situation?"

Again, this doesn't mean that we should be above conflicts, but it does mean that we need occasionally to ask the congregation if we are working on the right debate. I wonder if our church arguments don't serve a convenient function of distracting us from fulfilling the mission of Christ. On more than one occasion I've left a Worship Committee meeting, where we debated late into the night about some dopey idea I had, only to remember as I drove home Amos's warning that God is pretty much done with fancy worship services being constructed by those who do not do justice.

This brings us back to the necessity of the pastor entering the conflicts of the parish with a very specific job description. And that job is not simply to mediate between competing claims for the budget, or to develop a fair process for resolving the conflicting positions on the proposal to start a new contemporary worship service. And the job of the pastor is never to find consensus. Our job is to keep an eye out for the strange things the risen and ascended Christ is doing in the congregation, and in the world around it, and then lead the church toward it.

This type of leadership will, of course, also create conflicts. Even discerning where Christ is present and at work will create conflicts. And some of the conflicts will defy all good management strategies. But at least these conflicts are worth having.

X

Dollars and Sense:
A Practical Theology of Money

David Shinn

Can you imagine our world without poverty?

On July 6-8, 2005, as the G8 Summit was about to begin, another movement known as Live 8 launched its campaign in Philadelphia, with Bono as its main speaker. Live 8 hosted live concerts all across the globe from Philadelphia to Scotland to raise awareness of the ugly face of poverty that is affecting countless people worldwide. This incredible campaign to eradicate both poverty and AIDS is called ONE. Like Live Aid over twenty years ago, Live 8 and ONE are committed to rally the leaders and ordinary citizens of the G8 countries to save millions of lives in the poorest countries.

Moved by this audacious commitment to eradicate poverty and AIDS, the G8 leaders reached an unprecedented agreement: "$50 billion more a year in international assistance per year by 2010; AIDS drugs to all those who need it, and care for all AIDS orphans; primary schools for *all* children by 2015; a commitment to protect 85% of Africans against malaria; 100% debt cancellation for 18 of the world's poorest countries."[1] The leaders of ONE recognized that if the G8 nations live up to their promises, historic strides would be made in the fight against AIDS and poverty. They called for ONE to persist in pressuring

---

[1] http://one.org/About.html (accessed July 22, 2006)

the G8 nations to be sure that the promises are indeed fulfilled in 2006.

In my prayers, I express my hope to see this goal achieved in my lifetime, not as the fantasy of science fiction, but by the incredible real force of changed hearts.

What does it take to rid our world of poverty and AIDS? Money? Shifts of political power? Will money solve all of our problems? What does money mean to you? Is it just a tool? While working on this project, I met a college graduate who is working for the first time in her life. I asked her, "What is money?" She said to me, "For the first time in my life, money means more than just what my parents provide for me. It is a tool for me to meet the needs of my life, to provide opportunity to gather community and friendship, to celebrate what is important." As I sat there listening to her, I wanted to say, "Money is far more than that." Money is a tool that can bring transformation to our world. As a matter of fact, money can be a means for justice and hospitality.

In his recent book *What's Theology Got To Do With It?* Anthony Robinson raises the important connection between congregational practice and, consequently, personal practice, with theology. He writes:

> Theology has plenty to do with congregational health. Theological reflection is a way to align what we believe with who we are. Careful thinking about theology helps a congregation preach what it practices and practice what it preaches. If a congregation neglects core categories of faith, it is impossible for the congregation to become, in practice, something other than a faith community.[2]

---

[2] Robinson, Anthony B., *What's Theology Got To Do With It? Convictions, Vitality, and the Church* (Alban Institute, Herndon, VA), p. xi. Used by permission of the publisher.

What, then, is a theology of money? Now that's a can of worms that I'm not ready to open in a short essay. But at least we can all agree that the use, role and focus of money dominate a large portion of Jesus' teachings. In fact, next to his teachings on faith and practice, and death and resurrection, money was pretty much the other major subject. In fact, the issue of money has to do with one's devotion of mind, heart, and energy. "You cannot serve two masters!" Jesus said. Furthermore, the talk about money is not exclusively a concern of Christian scripture; it is a theme of the Hebrew scriptures as well. First, let us begin our construction of a theology of money by exploring how we understand money in relation to our faith. How does money function in our lives? How does money affect our lives and the lives of others? We may come to see money as a tool for justice and hospitality.

Embedded deeply in the Holiness Code of Leviticus is a sound theology of money. Leviticus 25 lifts up the concept and practice of Jubilee. Every seven years, the Israelites were to practice the sabbatical year, during which they were to allow their land and field to rest. Then on the seventh cycle of the seven-year cycle (the forty-ninth year), they were to sound the horn and proclaim aloud the year of Jubilee. In the Jubilee year, not only was the land to lay fallow, but debts were cancelled, acquired land returned, slaves freed, and economic balance once again restored. It is an incredible concept that allows those less fortunate in the years past to have an opportunity to start anew.

In 2000, Pope John Paul II encouraged nations, particularly the economic powers of the world, to cancel or lower debts of many struggling nations, thus allowing those nations an unprecedented opportunity to start new again. Such an act as lifted up by the Priestly writers, is an act of holiness: to forgive debts, to free bondage, and to give rest are acts of sacredness. The holiness of God penetrates daily life, work, family, worship and identity. Waldemar Janzen writes in his *Old Testament Ethics* that "Nowhere does the identity, in substance, between the priestly ethic and the familial ethic become more apparent than in Leviticus 25 with its provisions for the Sabbath year and the Jubilee year."[3] He connects the use of the land to the way of caring for the poor by saying, "The immediacy of the relationship of the land to Yahweh is striking. Israel is simply not to interfere. Just as the people are to belong to the Lord, so is the land (cf. v. 23).[4] Economic bondage can be viewed in completely new ways as we remember that we as well as the land belong to the Lord, Money can bring not only justice for the poor, but also hospitality to the disenfranchised.

Can you imagine our world if we practiced the year of Jubilee?

The year of Jubilee is like a divine reset button. It resets the concept of personal acquisition of wealth. It resets the capitalist order of the rich getting richer and the poor staying poor. It provides economic, political and communal refuge for those have been stricken with misfortune. It preserves resources. Imagine the relief it would offer to countries struggling underneath deep debt. Ninety percent of many African and Latin American countries' gross national product is devoted to paying off the debts to countries like our own. How can a government be able to get out of that slump while providing for its citizens? The year of Jubilee is a radical divine reset that would bring relief to more than we can imagine.

All the more, it is encouraging when we see money being used well. Warren Buffett, the second richest man in the world, gave the unprecedented amount of eighty-five percent of his $44 billion dollars to major charities. The Bill and Melinda Gates foundation is one of the five major beneficiaries of this radical generosity. The amount is staggering. Buffett gave over $35

---

[3] Waldemar Janzen, *Old Testament Ethic: A Paradigmatic Approach* (Westminster/John Knox Press, Louisville, KY, 1994), 116. Used by permission of the publisher.
[4] Ibid., 116.

billion dollars! His financial gift will enable the Bill and Melinda Gates foundation to fight epidemics and find new ways to tackle AIDS. What is even more amazing is that such an act of giving will inspire others to share their wealth in like manner as a means for justice and hospitality. God sure loves a cheerful giver! From the woman who offered up her two pennies to Warren Buffett offering up billions of dollars, we can be part of the revolution to bring changes through our economic means, translated into political force.

The revolution to stand boldly and live prophetically starts not with billions of dollars or larger than life figures such as Buffet and Gates, but it starts with you and me. In my current congregation, regular members became deeply concerned when they witnessed homeless people sleeping and finding refuge in the doorstep of the church. In 1980 the senior minister of the congregation, Rev. Dr. David Colwell, challenged the congregation by proclaiming that "one homeless person is one too many." With this cry for justice, a single individual bound together with others to form a living body called the Plymouth Housing Group (PHG), (http://www.plymouthhousing.org), an independent, non-profit organization that develops and operates housing for homeless and very poor people in Seattle.

PHG has since grown to be one of the largest providers of very low-income housing in downtown Seattle. With the challenge from their pastor and a generous response from the members, the church committed financially at first to purchase an abandoned building downtown. Then with a strong vision of revolution, the congregation organized itself with action teams, and on every weekend for the next few months they brought their hammers, drills, paint brushes, and most of all, their hearts, guided by a vision of people with housing and dignity. When the one building was ready for its tenants, the members were inspired to do more.

With more than 730 rental units and seventeen retail tenants in eleven buildings, PHG today has an annual operating budget of $7.2 million. The latest PHG project is building the very first geriatric care center and home for homeless people in our country. Where no city planners and government officials dared to dream, the citizens in this church were doing more than dreaming. They were engaged in helping to bring forth the vision of a world where poverty and homelessness will no longer be a reality. This is an inspiring vision that calls people to think and live differently. The revolution is not in some distant time and space; it is for here and now.

As a young pastor of this generation, I am inspired to make a difference by living that call for economic justice. I believe that vision is to be lived out first personally. If I am to inspire others to do live justly, I must live justly as well. In my congregation, we have a powerful and honest call to stewardship called "Each One Reach One." The Business Manager of the church, who functions much like a CFO for us, will organize all the givers of the church into categories and match one family to another family within the same giving categories. Then very prayerfully and pastorally, she sends the invitation for one family to meet another to talk about their stewardship practice in the past year and their commitment in the coming year. The two families, who may or may not know one another prior to this stewardship campaign, find a good time and place to meet. There they encourage one another to commit to the ministry vision of the new budget year by their financial commitment to the church. The pastors are not exempt from this process! We are matched up to another family of the church and invited to sit with that family, not as a pastor, but as fellow believers committing ourselves to the ministry vision for justice. The revolution begins first in our own hearts. Then from there, the Spirit can fan the flame to light others.

The single most prevalent subject dominating the Minor Prophets is justice, justice in the economic, political, and personal realms. After all, the political powers that be are responsible for the economic welfare of the least privileged

130

citizens of the land. Again and again, prophets like Hosea, Amos, and Micah challenge the royal governance and treatment of the poor. Ultimately, Micah asks, "He has told you, O mortal, what is good; and what does the Lord require of you, but to do justice, and to love kindness and to walk humbly with your God?" (6:8)

Our faith in a just God informs our lives and compels us to act justly. Money then becomes a tool for bringing internal faith into external action and practice! In our world, a "prosperity gospel" is being sold for millions, as in the case of Joel Osteen, who is being paid before he even speaks a word. Where is the justice in preaching a prosperity gospel when over sixty-five percent of the world is lacking just basic necessities of life? Why would God desire only for some to be rich? Is a prosperity gospel teaching that God destines for many to be poor? Such a view must be tested next to the call of the just God whose love is universal and unequivocal!   The incredible gift from people like Buffett and Gates will be the changing force for money to bring Jubilee for our changing world. Bono and the Live 8 organizers were right. If we can change hearts, we can change the world. Will you join the revolution?

Response by Lonnie Oliver
to David Shinn on Money

Recently, I saw the cover of two magazines that reminded me of a need for a theology of money. The first magazine was the October 2006 edition of *Reader's Digest*. There was a photograph of Marilyn Monroe in the top left corner on the front cover, but these large letter words grabbed my attention: "Your Money: 10 Ways to Keep More." Under these words was a larger roll of paper money with a rubber band around it. The second magazine that engaged my thinking about the theology of money was a *Money* magazine dated October 2006. Under the large letters of the word "Money" were these words in smaller print: "For you, your family, your future." In the middle of the front cover you could also read these words about a 43-page special report: "Retire Rich: How to Make Your Money Last a Lifetime."

In this self-centered, individualistic, materialist world, it is easy to understand the Latin proverb that says: "Money is either our master or our slave." We think that money provides status, security, and happiness. *However,* the apostle Paul says "For the love of money is a root of all kinds of evil. (1 Timothy 6:10) Money can be deceptive. It can be used to purchase things and to live a lifestyle beyond our means. The availability of credit allows us to temporarily satisfy our need for "conspicuous consumption" or to buy influence and/or power. In this consumer-oriented society, organized money has political power. It can influence votes on election day, or it can allow the rich to adopt poor black boys from Africa without providing nurture and care for a family so that it can remain intact. Why not use that money to preserve the family or to empower a village or a country? Money can open closed doors and shut doors that have remained open for years.

When it is your money, you want it to last a lifetime. No one wants to outlive their money. When you think it is yours, there is a tendency to want more and more. When oil companies make over three billion dollars in one quarter, it is a natural desire to want more money the next quarter. The success of a business is not judged by how humanitarian it has been, but rather, how much money it has brought in for any given quarter. In most cases, our personal success is based on our ability to bring in more and more money. When that does not occur, corporate positions are in jeopardy and we are considered a liability to that company. In this scenario, should our value be singularly based on our ability to create money, or in financial vernacular, increase market capitalization? With the uneven and inequitable distribution of wealth in our country, it is no secret that "the rich get richer and the poor get poorer."

As I look at problems of hunger, poverty and the spread of AIDS in Africa and among African-American females, and the exploitation of the natural resources on the continent of Africa and around the world, I can imagine a world without hunger, unnecessary death and poverty. I can imagine a world where people have enough food to eat, live in decent housing, receive adequate and appropriate healthcare and are judged by the content of their character and not by the color of their skin. In an ideal world, God's different gifts, cultures and spiritual expressions are affirmed and welcomed as beneficial and needed for all of God's creation. I glimpse God's Kingdom in the realm of creation right here on earth.

I appreciate the benevolent spirit of the G-8 Summit and Live 8 movement. It is great to know that people will use available resources to support the effort to address the issues of AIDS, poverty, hunger and healthcare. Money can be helpful in providing some immediate relief and assist in long-term transformation. However, I think that it will take more than

133

money to address poverty and other social issues. I believe that we need to affirm a theology of money that is based on a Biblical and theological understanding of stewardship. According to T.A. Kantonen:

> *Stewardship* is the English word used to translate the New Testament word *oikonomia*. The Greek word is a compound of *oikos*, meaning house, and *nomos*, meaning law. It refers thus to the management of a house or of household affairs … . The term acquires a spiritual significance, however, when our Lord uses it as a metaphor to describe a man's [sic] management of his whole life in responsibility to God.[1]

Stewardship calls attention to God as creator (Genesis 1) and humans as creatures created in the image and likeness of God to manage God's affairs. (Genesis 1:26) In other words, humans have been entrusted with time, talents, gifts and money to carry out God's will in all of God's creation. Humans are trustees who have a responsibility to God and God's creation. Therefore, theology of money is based on a theology of creation. God is the creator of all things and God has dominion over humans.

To understand and internalize this theology of money, one must understand the theology of creation and the theology of redemption. Humans were created to live in harmony with God's will and God's way. However, humans misused their freedom and rebelled against God. Humans stopped worshiping and serving the creator to fulfill their own needs and thus fell into sin. However, God had a redemption plan of love that was manifested through God's only begotten son, Jesus.

---

[1] From <u>A Theology of Christian Stewardship</u> by T.A. Kantonen copyright © 1956 Fortress Press. Used by permission of the publisher.

When we learn that God invites us to participate in bringing about the Kingdom of God on earth, then we understand that it is not our money, but a gift we share with all of God's creation for God's purposes. When we understand a theology of stewardship, we see money and all that God created for the common good. God has created adequate resources to take care of all God's creatures and creation. Greed and selfishness prevent us from seeing what God sees—love, justice and peace for everyone. The question becomes: "Will we see what God sees and join God in the renewal of God in creation for God's glory?"

XI

Distinguishing Ministry and Church Work: A Road Map to Healthy Ministry

William "Bill" A.C. Golderer

Let's begin with an unlikely phone conversation that yours truly was a part of several months back. It went something like this:

> Neal Presa (editor of this book project): Bill, it's Neal.
> Me: Hi Neal, what's up? Do you have that money you owe me?
> Neal: (Ignoring previous question) Hey, I am working on a book project and I need someone to work on a chapter on Self-Care and Pastoral Ministry and I thought of you.
> Me: (insert stunned silence)

It is hard to depict on the written page the deafening silence Neal must have heard in response to his suggestion. I have never thought of myself as particularly pulled together on this topic—unless it is one of those 'how-not-to-do' self-care chapters—I would be perfect for that; it was sort of an ironic twist to an otherwise serious book. Like many of my colleagues who are still grinding it out in their 30's, I have boundary issues between life and work. I love the ministry I do and it drives me nuts at the same time. While I dream about doing other, more lucrative things with my professional life, I thank God every day for meaningful work and good people to work alongside. So I am not exactly the poster-child for writing the chapter on self-care in that my life exhibits an infectious balance that colleagues notice and attempt to emulate. Hence the silence.

But my dis-ease with the topic goes beyond this. Even while Neal was speaking, I thought I should disqualify myself because the very words "pastoral self-care"' set off an involuntary eye-rolling episode as I began to recall what I remember of the literature out there. I don't think of myself as particularly cynical but I am more than a little wary of the various seminars, workshops, books, and articles I have come across that judicatories, colleagues and personnel committees offer up on the topic of ministerial self-care.

I attribute my wariness to the conviction that the scope and depth of the problem of ministerial fatigue, burnout, etc. is larger and more pernicious than the widely recommended remedies attempt to address. I contend that many of the practices don't deal with the root cause of the self-care crisis confronting pastors today. (Perhaps they never did). Many are content simply to suggest a reorientation of the pastor to her daily, monthly and annual routines, but they fail to challenge us to take a hard look to determine whether there is something about the way pastoral ministry is practiced in our post-Christendom, American marketplace context that needs a complete overhaul.

Overcoming Ambivalence on the Topic: Busting the clichés about Pastoral Self Care

While it has been said that clichés contain a grain of truth, sayings can also become clichés because they wear out from use. This is how I feel when I hear for the bajillionth time some of the mantras that promise renewal for the pastor "who does too much."

If I asked you, as someone who is likely either preparing for pastoral ministry or already engaged in it, to make a "top ten

137

list" of the most widely suggested practices of ministerial self care, I bet some of these would be on your list:

1. Listen to your inner voice when it says, "I am tired" and be sure to take a personal Sabbath every week
2. Whenever you say yes to something, you have to say no to something else.
3. Watch what you eat, drink eight glasses of water a day and eat more fruit.
4. Exercise regularly.
5. Pray.
6. Practice a discipline of twenty minutes of "fun" reading every day.
7. Sleep at least eight hours a night (?!).
8. Take long walks.
9. Decide on how you can incorporate play into your routine.
10. Schedule spiritual renewal retreats for yourself at least twice a year.

The list of suggestions goes on. I don't want to be misunderstood. There is not a thing wrong with any of these suggestions. Much of it is prudent advice for congregants and pastors alike. How might our congregations change if everyone covenanted to get at least eight hours of sleep or, if they haven't, stay home from committee meetings?

It isn't enough to ask about any individual's practices. Beginning to address the crisis of ordained ministers leaving the church will require looking more deeply at the issues that lie behind the need for a better diet, taking a personal Sabbath, and becoming better at saying no.

A Generational Thing? Where Did All My Peers Go?

My own anecdotal experience is not a good substitute for a credible research study about the retention rate of young people staying in pastoral ministry in the mainline Protestant enterprise. However, it does inform my perspective.

I had nine close friends in my graduating class from seminary, eight of whom were headed for ordination (in a variety of denominations) and looking forward to service in the parish. Of those eight, I am the last one standing. It is a frightening statistic and it gives me pause. Where have they gone? Why have they gone and to what other callings?

The reasons are as varied as the individuals involved. But there is a thread running through the stories of these bright, young, talented, passionate and selfless people who decided pastoral ministry wasn't what they wanted. I can give you a window into what I think is going on by sharing one of their stories.

Leaving a Pastoral Gig In Order to Practice Ministry

With the permission of a close friend, I share this story. This pastor is frustrated with her place of call. Her hours are incredibly long. The congregational expectations for performance are exceedingly high. Her remunerative compensation is embarrassingly low. While all of this had been hard to deal with, it hasn't caused her seriously to consider leaving pastoral ministry. She just felt as though it came with the calling. But recently there has been something nagging at her that has made her wonder if she can stay with it.

She served alongside four other colleagues in a large, affluent suburb, the kind of church others admire from afar and wonder how nice it would be to labor in a field with so many resources. Recently she asked me if I had time for coffee. She said she had a breakthrough idea about how she could continue in ministry and not give into the resentment she had been feeling about her professional duties. Her idea grew out of an invitation from the congregation's personnel committee. The committee had alerted her that the church's administrative assistant was leaving to take another job. Members of the committee wondered whether she would meet with them as they developed a new job description. Of course, she said she would.

When she perused the draft of the administrative assistant position, she had an epiphany that hit her like a ton of bricks. The job called for skills in the creation and maintenance of efficient systems, modest proficiency with computers, good organizational skills, yada yada. The expectation was a Monday to Friday, 9am to 5pm, 40 hour work-week. The compensation package was fair (in fact only $3,000 less than she was currently making) and, as it turned out, a better health benefits package than she received through the denomination.

She invited me to coffee to test out her idea. What did I think about her resigning her ordained pastoral position in the church and working instead as the administrative assistant?

After a lot of prayer and reflection, my friend realized that it wasn't the long hours that depressed her. It wasn't the workload or even the unrealistic expectations of excellence without having adequate resources to do things excellently. It wasn't the dismal pay. These things may be hard to deal with but were not something that would lead her to question her calling.

None of what she did, she said, had to do with discipleship as much as with maintaining the smooth running of a religious non-profit organization. She knew she had gifts in this area. People affirmed her much of the time. But she wondered if this is what Jesus Christ had called her to do in order to make what she called a "kingdom difference."

She described the sense of being awakened from this ministerial grind to realize that while she had become excellent at doing "church work," she wasn't willing to continue much longer without doing the ministry she felt called to do: work that made an impact on the lives of people whom she met, work that was deeply integrated with her understanding of what it means to follow Christ's call to discipleship. She thought about the artists we knew who would take a "day job" in order to pay the bills and help make ends meet so that they could devote themselves to their art in the off hours. My friend was convinced she could unlock her passion for ministry by working for the church during the day and then tackling her call to ministry after hours.

It is sobering to think that a pastor who has devoted time and financial resources to theological education, met an untold number of judicatory requirements, sacrificed much in the way of a personal life, and agreed to a comparatively low salary in order to pursue a call to ministry might then leave it after just a few years. It gave me pause to hear that so much of her life was devoted to "church work" that she felt she had to get out of the pastoral role in order to be liberated to "do ministry."

Church Work vs. Ministry: What's the Difference?

Make no mistake. All jobs, from the mundane to the thrilling, contain aspects that are not "sexy." There are budget numbers to crunch; there are expense reports to file; there are meetings to sit through that stray far from the agenda and careen off into a million dizzying directions. Pastoral ministry is no exception to this reality, as we know all too well.

In addition to this, there are a number of things I never learned in seminary that would be expected of me, such as competency in collecting estimates on a fatigued furnace, reserving vans for the youth mission trip, overhauling committee organizational structures, and so on. Doing such tasks with one's whole heart can, of course, be ministry. Sometimes what seem like mundane interactions with people whilst tending to these chores are actually opportunities for mysterious encounters with God.

I am not suggesting that one look for a pastoral position that liberates pastors totally from parts of a job they deem tedious. But I think there is a delicate "ph balance" that needs to be achieved and maintained between doing the things that make a church run well and doing things that make a difference in people's lives.

I have a simple tool that I have used to test the "ph balance" in my own pond for ministry. In order to develop this test, I have adapted a distinction I read once in a book by Harvard Business School leadership guru, Ron Heifitz. He claimed that while managers do things the *right way*, leaders determine *what the right things are* to do. Often, pastoral ministry consumes me with the challenge of doing the things in front of me as efficiently and as excellently as I can. Sometimes though, time needs to be set aside to ask: *are these the right things for me to be doing*? Is this what God has called me to this place to do and be and become in this place for these people?

For me self-care in the pastorate begins with attention to the "ph balance" of asking the leadership questions: am I being a good steward of my passion, my creativity, my love for church members and those on the edges of faith in the community? I can do all of the self-care work in the world but if I do not attend to this macro line of questioning, I put myself in greater risk of disappointment, burnout and perhaps an early exit from ministry than a thousand missed walks, renewal retreats, or personal Sabbath days.

I am not ruling out performing the mundane tasks of ministry with intentionality. Or taking a personal Sabbath. Eat your berries and granola while taking a wander in the woods. But while you are at it, take an inventory of how much of your workday is spent feeding the insatiable appetite of the institutional monster and how much has anything to do with what you understand the Holy Spirit is calling you to do.

For too many of my colleagues, the ph level on this measurement is anything but balanced. They feel as though there is a minimum set of expectations that are laid out in terms of making sure things run smoothly. If there is any time left over it can be devoted to proactive study, prayer with others, or embarking upon initiatives they feel God has placed on their heart.

Must I Resign? Correct, Don't Compensate

I am convinced that ordained pastoral ministry can be bliss or torture and often it is both. But for many of my colleagues, the feeling of being mired in expectations to make a program or congregation as a whole run smoothly and grow steadily leads to a feeling of hopelessness. They feel trapped and they can't see pastoral ministry for what I believe it is. Depending on the context, pastoral ministry can contain the ingredients for the most exciting, creative, nimble, caring, meaningful work there is.

So what if you feel stuck? Must you leave and start over with a new congregation? Must you leave altogether? Maybe. But I frequently consult some wisdom I received as far back as Little League. As advice, it is deceptively simple—but not simplistic.

Too often, our struggles to maintain this ph balance are understood as "solo" work. If you find yourself feeling drained, many pastors I know feel like they need to make the adjustments, pull back on their work, and employ the conventional wisdom of the self-care gurus without looking to correct the core of the problem alongside members of their community. This may work well for some. But I would like to suggest to the coming generation of ministers that they embark upon a journey of candor and collaboration with their community's leadership that keeps the leadership-management distinction in the foreground at all times. It is not just a matter of

143

doing something in the right way, but of having the wisdom to discern what is the right thing to do. Such wisdom is the work of the whole community.

Are we concerned with executing quality programs, running a tight ship, growing numerically, and reversing downward trends at the expense of listening for direction from God? What is it that ignites our passion for ministry, steels our commitment to the long haul, and makes the long walks and granola a value-added to our diet rather than a life-or-death self-care tactic enabling us to hang in another year in the hopes something will change?

Monitoring the ph balance between church work and ministry in the ecosystem of one's particular pond is hard work. Acting collaboratively but also decisively to alter it when it skews toward church work (at the expense of ministry) requires honesty, courage and humility. Pastoral self-care that relies on techniques without giving attention to these fundamental questions will not lead anyone to a more fulfilling, more faithful ministry or, for that matter, to a more vital witness to Jesus Christ.

Response by Deborah van deusen Hunsinger to Bill Golderer on Healthy Ministry

A few years ago I was asked to lead a three-day workshop on "Self-care for Pastors" at Con-Ed (the Continuing Education program at Princeton Theological Seminary). I was glad to say "yes" because I wanted to offer whatever support I could to young pastors, for all the reasons Bill Golderer recites. I was relieved that I could give the workshop during our Fall Reading Week, so that I wouldn't have to juggle the seminar with my regular teaching duties. Yet by the time late October rolled around, I was exhausted. I had heavy administrative responsibilities that year and some writing deadlines bearing down on me. The irony didn't escape me that, desperately in need of rest and rejuvenation, I was offering a course on self-care.

The struggle for adequate self-care has been a constant during the thirty years of ministry that have followed my graduation from seminary in 1976. Sometimes the struggle has been intense—as when my first year of full-time seminary teaching coincided with a misdiagnosed illness that led to life-threatening anemia. Sometimes it is only the subliminal *basso continuo* of weighing every single decision: "If I spend an hour writing this letter of recommendation, I won't have time to call my mother this evening; if I stop to listen to this student now, I won't have time to finish preparing my lecture before class." (The perceptive reader will have noticed that this practice corresponds with Bill's #2 suggested practice of ministerial self-care: "Whenever you say yes to something, you have to say no to something else.") As far as practical tips go, I don't know any habit of mind as helpful—or finally as disheartening—as this one.

145

Yet what I value about Bill's essay is that it cuts to a much deeper level of analysis than any individual's habits of mind or lifestyle. It addresses systemic and cultural questions about how ministry is practiced in this country. What are our expectations of our pastors? How can any single human being possibly live up to such (unrealistic) expectations?

Why did Bill's friends leave the ministry? His anecdotal case study presents a friend who devised a plan to leave the pastorate so that she could pursue her true calling: ministry itself. I wanted to scream, laugh and cry all at the same time. It is heartrending to imagine that such a plan would improve this pastor's lot. I know something about the rigors of seminary training, the sacrifices involved, the courage, perseverance and vision it takes to go the long haul through all the requirements, both academic and ecclesial. All that to become an administrative assistant?

Yes, sacrifice it all; throw it all overboard in an instant if it means being able to do real ministry, to be involved with things that really matter, to be involved with people who matter eternally, essentially. "Am I being a good steward, of all that God has given me: passion, creativity, love?" Bill asks. "Am I actually doing what God has called me to do?" If you can answer that question with a joyful "yes," you will have found the wellspring that will sustain you year in and year out.

From the direction his essay takes, I am imagining that Bill advised his friend to combine her personal gifts of discernment with some forthright conversation about her unhappiness. "Correct, don't compensate." "Correct the core of the problem alongside members of the community." "Embark on a journey of candor and collaboration" about what you are truly called to do. This sounds like very good advice to me.

In the concluding chapter of his book, *Self-Care*, Ray Anderson writes:

146

Self-care is not a project to be undertaken by the self alone. The core of the self is grounded in relation with another, or others. The picture of the solitary Adam in Genesis 2 is one of self-alienation rather than self-fulfillment ... . The divine image is not a religious quality of the individual person, but a spiritual reality expressed through the interchange of persons in relation. The sharing of our feelings with those whom we trust to listen and respond is the beginning of self-care.[1]

Bill's friend, in my opinion, was practicing excellent self-care when she invited Bill out for coffee. We are not meant to discern God's calling all by ourselves; it is a communal project from beginning to end, and at every step along the way. The church is a single body made up of many members, each one of which is essential to the working of the whole. *Self-care, paradoxically, is not something that we can provide for ourselves; it is something that we can only receive from others as a gift.*

That is the crux of why Bill's hypothetical "top ten list," on giving yourself the care you need finally falls short. Look at it again:

1. Listen to your inner voice when it says, "I am tired" and be sure to take a personal Sabbath every week.
2. Whenever you say yes to something, you have to say no to something else.
3. Watch what you eat, drink eight glasses of water a day and eat more fruit.
4. Exercise regularly.
5. Pray.

---

[1] Ray S. Anderson, <u>Self-Care: A Theology of Personal Empowerment and Spiritual Healing</u> (Wheaton, Illinois: Victor Books, 1995), p. 238. Used by permission of the author – Dr. Ray S. Anderson, Senior Professor of Theology and Ministry, Fuller Theological Seminary, Pasadena, CA.

6. Practice a discipline of twenty minutes of "fun" reading every day.
7. Sleep at least eight hours a night (?!).
8. Take long walks.
9. Decide on how you can incorporate play into your routine.
10. Schedule spiritual renewal retreats for yourself at least twice a year.

With the exception of #5, all of these suggestions are oriented toward what the individual can do for him- or her- self. Eat, sleep, relax, play, read, walk. Even "pray" ceases to be the dialogue it is meant to be if all that we do is ask God for help with our updated list of things to do.

The most important self-care practice I know is to gather regularly with a group of fellow Christians to talk in confidence about your life, your work, your failures, your misgivings, your challenges and your joys. Building a community of trust is the very heart of the task of self-care. "Ministry is dangerous," writes Margaret Kornfeld, "for those who are disconnected from themselves."[2] Ministers may be starving spiritually and not know it. When they are absorbed in the lives of others, they can easily lose track of their own lives and not know how to ask for what they need.

Like all human beings, what pastors need is the companionship of those whom they respect and trust. They need a place to let their hair down, to confess their sins, to ask for help. They need to meet at the intersection of God and community, where they can be strengthened by the faith and wisdom of others. Such mutual giving and receiving in the life of faith is what we were made for. "The eye cannot say to the hand,

---

[2] Excerpt from Cultivating Wholeness: A Guide to Care and Counseling in Faith Communities © 1998 by Margaret Zipse Kornfeld (New York: Continuum, 1998), p. 282. Used by permission of the publisher. See especially Chapter Ten: Tending Yourself, pp. 282-305.

"I have no need of you," nor again the head to the feet, "I have no need of you." (1 Corinthians 12:21) Our relationships with each other are the means through which God cares for us and through which we practice true self-care. This essay is dedicated with gratitude to all the groups that have shepherded me through thirty years of ministry: from case consultation groups to spiritual direction groups, from my women's prayer group to my nonviolent communication practice groups: "You are the body of Christ and individually members of it."

XII

Epilogue:
Where Do We Go From Here?

Mienda Uriarte

One of the more enjoyable jobs I completed during my tenure with the Office of Youth and Young Adult Ministries was consulting with groups of individuals from congregations, middle governing bodies, and ministry organizations. Most of them requested my counsel regarding the integration or inclusion of young adults (18-39 years) into the life of the group. The Presbyterian Church (U.S.A.) has long been struggling with this particular challenge, and GenXers have been proving to be more enigmatic than previous generations of young adults. So, together we embarked on a journey. Earlier in my term, during the course of my time with one particular group, I encountered a response that went something like this, "This generation is just too difficult. I think we will just let this one pass and wait until the next one comes along." Little did I know at the time that I would encounter this response quite frequently. Sometimes it was accompanied with strong emotion and other times it was uttered with a resigned calm. Either way, I was always surprised—surprised that the conclusion to dismiss an entire generation was completely acceptable.

As I read each of the chapters of this book I was reminded of what a huge mistake that would be. Each of the essays presented by my colleagues is smart, innovative, and creative. The thoughtful and courageous posture of challenging the status quo, standing adverse and strong in the face of orthodoxy, or articulating a creedal stance with brilliance is

150

evidence of leaders who are forging paths and are influencing directions for the church in the 21st century.

The present and future church calls for change. None of us can pretend to have a crystal ball and know exactly what the denomination will look like in the future, but we do know that it must change. The cultures of the globe challenge us to be authentic and relevant and that means that we must be adaptive and flexible and open to doing and being in ways that deviate from the usual. The Presbyterian Church (U.S.A.), like all mainline Protestant denominations in the United States, must understand herself in several contexts simultaneously—as a connectional denomination throughout the country, as a sister church in full communion with other denominations, and as a component of Christianity in a world where the majority is comprised of other religions, and so forth. And, I hear my sisters and brothers calling us to that place of honest assessment as they write and express their concerns and hopes. I hear them reminding us all that our vision cannot be myopic because we live in a world that is expansive.

The Moderator of the Central Committee of the World Council of Churches, His Holiness Aram I, recently addressed the gathering in Brazil. He challenged the churches, gathered in the spirit of the one true and living God, by saying that "We in the 21st Century must find fresh forms of expression, new avenues to overcome divisions, and inspiring vision that spiritually engages the churches and its members in this calling. That can happen, in my judgment, only by confronting our 'brutal facts.'"[1]

I'll offer three questions—certainly among many others—that I believe we must honestly face in order to seek a future in this century that will be filled with hope and promise:

---

[1] "The Future of the Church in the 21st Century" symposium hosted by His Holiness, Aram I, Moderator of the Central Committee of the World Council of Churches, February 10, 2006.

1. Will we be inclusive or institutionally protective?
2. Will we be driven fundamentally by spiritual vision or organizational momentum?
3. Will we seek "incremental change" or "deep change" in pursuing this future?

The very same core values outlined in the questions listed above are also woven throughout the articles included in this book—inclusivity, spirituality, and depth.

From my own "location" (gender, ethnicity, culture, generation, etc.), as I find myself in any variety of situations and circumstances, I try consistently to ask the question, whose voices are being heard? And, by deduction, whose voices are being neglected? Whose voices need to be given special standing in order to insure their place in the conversation? This project, in and of itself, is a way of doing just that. It's a way of giving voice to a generation of leaders who would too easily be passed over and dismissed without a second thought. The active contribution by these pastors is their way of proclaiming their place at the Table, for which we should all be grateful.

In an amateur article reviewing a movie of this past summer, "The Da Vinci Code" (film content goes according to Dan Brown's book, *Da Vinci Code*, and the story tells about detective hunting in our times but the main issue is, as we know, approximately 2000 years old), the reviewer honestly states, "I would say even though we live in a post-modern world and mostly in post-Christian societies, there is still a strong desire to find the spiritual values and a trustful orientation for our personal lives."[2] This person doesn't expand this statement in any way, but I thought it poignant that a casual web posting would throw this avowal out to the cyberspace travelers perhaps

---

[2] www.emaxhealth.com "Da Vince Code: the Modern Spirituality Needs Healing"

152

to pick up on their way and ruminate on at some point. On a far less casual tone and with much more thought and intent, my colleagues have consistently pointed to the need for lifting up the spiritual nature and spirituality component in all things pertinent to our lives. Whether it's considering the role of money or prayer, self-care or conflict management, the element of spirituality is without question.

Hand in hand with the matter of spirituality, there is the question of depth. GenXers do not want to waste time on the superficial. In this case the demand for authenticity is a demand for the church to go deeper into anything and everything deemed necessary for consideration. A CBS news poll found that 82 percent of Americans surveyed said that they profess a belief in God. But the same poll also found that nearly a third of those surveyed believes traditional religions are out of date. "If you're dealing with people in their 20s and 30's, being relevant to them and their world and the future they face is going to mean changes. It's not like we have our church life over here and a social and political life over there. We're saying, no, these things are integrated and we want to live this out in an integrated way."[3] This philosophy is more than a theory – it's a call to action. As Liz describes the intentional community model utilized by Covenant Community Church, she unabashedly declares that they could have opted for several other ways to live out Christian community, but they didn't. The other ways might have given them a better statistical profile that may have made for a better looking annual report. Instead, they opted for the model that would provide members of each of the communities a more substantive, a more meaningful connection to each other and to the Holy.

As I said earlier, who knows what the future holds for the organization of our denomination? Who knows where the

---

[3] CBS News, "Christianity, in 21st Century Clothes" by Lee Cowan, April 13, 2006

postmodern era will lead? And will the emerging churches finally be fully revealed? Any one of these conversations will potentially take us in a million different directions. And, while I'm skeptical with some of the possible answers to any of these questions, I am confident that the greater value is of those with whom the conversation will be had. The relationships we have with one another and the willingness to engage those of a dismissed generation mean more to the community of Christ than any academic argument we might have.

And so, I am eternally grateful to each of the authors of this project—those who willingly took the risk in letting themselves be heard as well as those who responded with grace and faithfulness. May the Spirit of God's Shalom continue to thrive in each and every one of you. Amen.

Appendix I

In 1999 at the Stony Point Conference Center in New York, the first of the 7% Events convened, gathering young adult ministers for mutual enrichment and worship. Dubbed 7% to indicate that of the total number of Ministers of Word and Sacrament serving in a parish setting in the Presbyterian Church (U.S.A.) only 7% were under the age of 40, the Event asked conference participants to name their "Top 10 Things I wished I learned at seminary but didn't."

The results of the two most recent 7% Young Clergy Conferences—New Orleans, LA (2003) and San Francisco, CA (2005)—are published below and quoted in their entirety as they were received. Due to budgetary constraints, the 7% event, formerly a PC(U.S.A.)-sponsored event, joined other ecumenical partners to have a Young Adult Pastors Event; the first of these was held in the Fall 2007.

The Editor, who served on the planning teams for both the 2003 and 2005 events, is grateful to the Rev. David Shinn for his assistance in compiling the results.

(Editor's Note: An editorial decision was made not to edit out any of the comments and feedback received from conference participants. While some comments may read comical and facetious, there is a profound element of truth contained within those comments, expressing the need of that particular young adult minister as he/she came to the 7% for refreshment and encouragement)

Top 10 Results from 7% Young Clergy Conference
@ New Orleans, October 2003

Personal Clergy Finance	"how to file taxes as clergy"(4) "personal financial responsibilities"
Negotiating Financial Call	"housing allowance options" "manse" "equity accrual" "shared equity" "how to negotiate the salary, social security offset, estimated tax payments" "particularly for a single woman" "interview skill" "how to navigate the board of pension"(3) "interview skill" "overall call process"
Church Budget and Finance	"how to read and plan a budget"(16) "stewardship campaigns"(4)
Self Care	"how to deal with clergy killers"(3) "taking time to be with those who love you" "developing passion for ministry" "single minister issues" "pay attention to how satisfied you are" "time management" "you can't please everyone" "confidential places to vent/share/pray are a must" "self care is very important"(4) "how to relate to other clergy" "sustaining/maintaining/enhancing spiritual disciplines"(2) "the importance of having a pastoral therapist"

	"dealing with personal authority issues; exerting pastoral authority to different generations" "preventing burn out"(3) "how to make the most of your vacation and study leaves" "I don't need to be all things to all people; there are people who will care for me" "the value of setting limits"(3) "claiming ministerial identity" "ministry makes fat" "how to keep Sabbath"(22) "I wish I'd known myself better in seminary" "I wish I'd spent more time reflecting on vocation (ministry verses management of church as a business" "how to discern where God is calling you?" "there is a good and exciting life after the seminary"
Value Self as Theologians	"how few people would actually care what Calvin thinks or the Confessions say" "value and treasure theological community" "understand the theological education is only the beginning – more to learn from the community" "the joy, the struggle and the importance of not only thinking theologically, but being aware of and sensitive to cross-cultural issues and dynamics – and how that affects us as well" "understanding what it means to be 'always being reformed' as well as Reformed tradition"(3) "prayer life is as important as theological thinking" "theological education continues after

	seminary" "the importance of reading the bible daily" "how to be a clergy couple" "I wish I had known that my seminary had no clue what was important to actual churches" "stronger con ed courses for the first 5 years " "more spiritual formation and pastoral care courses"(5)
Management of Ministry	"strategies for redevelopment"(4) "conflict management skills"(20) "how to lead a small church"(2) "the importance of finding a mentor"(4) "liturgical theology; Taize worship, praise and worship, funeral, wedding, Eucharist, and baptism"(4) "developing leadership"(12) "elder and deacon training" "ideas/info on some of the basic PC(USA) journals, etc. and other resources that help with worship, planning, issues, events, etc."(5) "how to lead a staff meeting" (and staff dynamic) (7) "how to create an effective ministry team"(2) "how to moderate a session meeting"(11) "denominational services, being Presbyterian, education, conventionalisms"(9) "how to deal with multi-staff dynamics" e.g., "that the associate always loses" (10) "church life cycles and how to deal with dying churches" "how to be an effective communicator" "evangelism skills" "pastoral presence" "the Stephen Ministry motto" "how and when to change a church practice

	that isn't theologically sound" "committee management" "how to effect change in healthy and positive ways" "extended practical ministry" "urban ministry issues" "how to generate a positive stewardship in the church" "gift discernment" "what to do with walk-ins who ask for help" "value on basic ministry skills, i.e., preaching, worship, sacrament"(4) "value continuing education" "organizational/administrative aspect of running a church"(3) "youth ministry skills" "time management"(2) "developing a vision"(2) "understanding the benefit of internship" "working with non-Presbyterian members" "how to create and recognize a healthy congregation" "understanding theology and awareness of music" "fostering community in ourselves and our congregation" "understanding the joy of caring for a congregation" "how to be more discerning of different types of people (a lot of nuts out there)" "anticipating generational, cultural/ communal issues" "integrating business aspect of the church with the spiritual side of the faith" "how to know when to end a call"

159

	"end of life choices/medical decisions" "how to give children's sermons"(3) "basics on theology of other denomination" "tools to set helpful feed back from the congregation or personnel committee" "church liability, lawsuits, background check skill" "BOP and the formula of agreement" "grief and healing"(2) "longevity in ministry" "how to perform the sacraments or stronger sacramental theology in my education" "the intersection between churches and media/popular cultures/technology"(4) "various different worshipping traditions and styles"(6) "ministry is hard" "I wish I learned about how to teach a class" "pre-marital counseling skills"(3)

Conference participants held a morning open forum "Talk Back with Dr. Phil" about their needs in ministry and what they would like seminaries to do. Rev. Dr. Philip Butin, president and professor of theology at San Francisco Theological Seminary, served as one of the keynote speakers of the New Orleans event. He moderated the discussion. The feedback of participants is below:

- self integration
- balance of theories and practices
- feeling of cheap labor in internship; carrying it over to the parish
- wish the seminary has a stronger sense where the church is; faith, congregational situation; rather than focusing on how the church should be

- disappointing for first call (about 20-25%)
- identifying systemic dysfunctions in the church and being part of the power and principalities
- internship, early on in the seminary training
- seminary professors need to spent more time in church; they should be planted in the church from time to time
- feedback loop from the pastors to the seminary to be the pastor in resident
- have first call support programs,
- politics of grant
- the ministries of the Synod; understanding different cultural experiences, i.e. Nebraska
- professors making classes practical,
- value of staying in church a long time
- discerning how long to stay in a church; based on our own needs, sense of limit, stamina
- kenotic theology in pastoral ministry—relying on what God provides for the work of the ministry while at the same time ridding ourselves of what maybe beneficial
- annually negotiating a covenant between the church and the pastor
- wondering about longevity in ministry
- anger, stress management, anxiety, conflict management, more in-depth pastoral care and counseling to address these issues.
- prepare seminarians to serve in diverse settings, settings of diversity
- before turning the wheels to change an institution, we need to listen to the Navigator.

Top 10 Results from 7% Young Clergy Conference
@ San Francisco, October 2005

How to prepare clergy taxes!

How to do church administration

How to pastor churches that are NCDs or non-traditional faith communities

How to encourage and support others in ministry

How to nurture your own spiritual life

How to read the Bible as a spiritual seeker rather than as a scholar

How to pray and how to teach others to pray

How to advertise and market your church or programs in the 21st century

How to lead Session meetings

How to work with volunteers

How to lead a capital campaign

Rental/space use in urban contexts—perhaps real estate training would help!

Delve in traditions that know how to manage and resolve guilt and self-recrimination

Conflict management in politically-charged entities, likes sessions, boards of deacons, and Presbyterian women's groups!

Understanding gossip as a clear, prevalent acceptable means of communication, how to interpret its underlying messages, and how to tell juicier stories to seed the grapevine toward ministry

Owning a particular book does not mean you possess its knowledge, unless you actually read, reflect, and apply it.

It's okay to not know what you're doing

Negotiating terms of call to your advantage, rather than as a misguided attempt at humility that will resurface as resentment later

Location, location, location

Institutional racism connected to individual racism

Leading a graveside service as well as a funeral

Moderating meetings

Negotiating terms of call

Personal self-care and spiritual growth, spiritual disciplines and practices

Deacon and elder training

Pre-marital counseling (content, structure)

Funeral preparation (actually observing one, if we haven't; learning basic process of arrangements with funeral home, family, etc.)

Baptism class (content, structure) for adults as well as parents

Understanding church budgets—general (% to staff, mission, etc., ... big picture understanding)

Understanding church finances—e.g. does pastor know who tithes? (pro/cons for this); stewardship campaigns (what are they and why important)

Setting up a mission team (general principles of training) and follow-up ideas

Old Testament and New Testament classes and history taught with an eye toward what people really want to know in the pew (i.e. why it matters that Joseph went to Nazareth instead)

Running a capital campaign

Working with nominating committees

Hiring and firing church employees

Conflict management in a spiritual context

Techniques to inspire mission giving in the church and methods to accomplish them

Sabbaticals

Grant writing

Developing spiritual gifts of congregation members

Visual presentations with sermons

Developing health ministries in the local church

Recruiting volunteers! [double emphases is participant's]

Understanding budgets

How to run committees

An understanding of redevelopment/revitalization

Stewardship!!   How to teach, preach and run effective campaigns

Session moderation—Robert's Rules of order

Self-Care –how to manage time—take time away from work

Empowering individuals

More training in educating children in the faith

Children sermons!!! [emphasis is participant's]

Basic building maintenance—plumbing, roofing, setting mouse traps, etc.

How to work with music directors (how to read music)

Spiritual self-care and balance during weeks when you have 3 meetings a day, the sermon is disjointed and someone dies, etc.

How to deal pastorally with church members who become friends

How to answer inappropriate personal questions asked of you by members of the congregation

How to manage staff

How to be with a church and help it die—from discernment that it should close, to the end

How to go "digital' with worship, office procedures, websites, etc.

How do bridge generations in the church

Actual baptism and Lord's Supper "practice" perhaps like a CPR Training Day

How to repair cars that you can afford as pastor

Selecting songs in worship that everybody likes and knows, but also adding new ones

Speaking Spanish

Creating stained glass

Piano tuning—seriously on this one

Re-roofing 40ft. high A-frame churches

Organ maintenance

How to deal with salt water and anointing

How to get potlucks and social hours to be healthier

The inherent loneliness that is a part of ministry—being able to be prepared for it and handle it in healthy ways

How to run a finance meeting

Long-range plan

How to effectively serve as head of staff when you're the youngest on staff

Pastoring and parenting—how to not sacrifice your family for the church but also be as good and faithful pastor as you can

How to get a jam out of the copier—just kidding, sort of [participant's humor]

Seminary did not prepare me for the isolation of being a pastor (but not one in a bubble)

Seminary did not prepare me to be a politician, accountant, set dresser, costume maker, restauranteur, suicide prevention specialist, baker, lawyer, psychoanalyst, or Jeff Probst or Martha Stewart

Seminary did not prepare me the amount of really bad Christian music with poor theology and pop

Seminary did not remotely prepare me to clone myself!

Seminary did not prepare me for people who have boundary issues and refuse to accept my limitations

Seminary did not prepare me for adults that act like children and think I'm their favorite babysitter

Seminary did not prepare me to deal with male overtures and well meaning proposals to date someone's sibling, friend or any other person that needs someone really nice

Seminary did not prepare me to appreciate fully the heat containment properties of a black polyester velvet robe in the full of summer

Seminary did not prepare me for everyone assuming that every gift card or poster I receive for the rest of my life has to have a biblical verse or a cross on it (or bizarre gifts like crowns of thorns, etc. made of plastic resin or that glow in dark)

Seminary did not prepare me to fix furnaces, air conditioners, 20 year-old televisions, gas stoves, dishwashers, toilets, pianos, or 400 lb. doors (or sound systems and projectors, or copy machines or to pray for any of these things to work)

How to pastor a church in the 21st century

How to manipulate a session meeting using Jedi-mind control

How to say "Tuna casserole, mmm ... delicious" and sound like you really mean it.

How to summarize the complexities of Reformed theology into a sound-bite that will fit on a bumper-sticker

How to climb off a spiritual pedestal when no one will give you a ladder

The answer to deep spiritual questions like "what color should we paint the nursery?"

How to politely say, "Would someone please remove that screaming baby from the sanctuary"

The importance of turning off the lavalier mic before using the bathroom

How to fix copy machine paper jams

The mind-numbing madness known as Presbytery meetings

Bizarre dynamics between pastors and associates, especially when the pastor is a man and the associate is not!

Assessing church dynamics (checking yourself and the congregation)

Exegeting a parish, especially when discerning whether or not one is called to serve in a specific parish

Dealing with church financial statements

Strategies for dealing with heads of staff who are "creative" with Presbyterian polity (I'm on my second; periodic polity refresher courses would be helpful for those of us who serve in polity-challenged congregations!)

How to dress as a young woman minister (guys have it easy!)

How to justify clergy self-care in the face of a burned out head of staff who is from a different generation and won't take care of himself

What to do when your head of staff only works 3 hours a day and wants to spend an hour of that time shooting the breeze in the associate's office

How to deal with a toxic (i.e. insulting and unhappy) person who is married to your head of staff (I'm on my second)

Creative, experiential worship. Everything I learned about this was extracurricular and haphazard. Congregations need more than the BCW.

Moderating a Session meeting

Financial planning

Stereotypical ministerial expectations as keys to success and failure: "They don't care how much you know until they know how much you care."

How to work when your church is healthy, operating out of budget surplus, growing and experiencing no major crisis or divisions

How to take and enjoy a day off

How different is your church from seminary, identifying the theological context of those you serve

How "defining your pastoral identity" is really just being yourself (that thing you avoided on ordination exams)

How to "preach" instead of presenting the homiletical application of the exegetical process (How important is personality/charisma to preaching)

How sarcasm may be used to communicate effectively

How to enjoy Taizé

How to avoid making definitive statements (in writing) when tired.

Strategic planning/mission statements

Transformational ministry

Taxes/finances

Funerals/weddings

Family Systems Theory

How to balance family/church/me

How to deal with difficult people

The nuts and bolts of the financial workings of a church—church an audit is and how it is done, what the jobs of treasurer and financial secretary involve, how to read financial report, etc.

I don't think seminary prepared me very well for moderating a session. I would've appreciated practicing with a mock session, even pretending to be an elder to see what a meeting is like from that side of things.

How to handle authority as a young pastor when so much of church is old enough to be my grandparents.

The nuts and bolts of stewardship—the different ways you can do a stewardship program. I don't ever remember talking about raising money.

Which brings be to negotiating a salary package. I needed more information on how to do that, not just what to ask for but how to ask for it.

Planning—long-term and short-term

Team ministry—building teams and small groups

Creative worship

Spiritual disciplines—centering prayer, body work, healing

Self-care

Time management

Global issues

Justice ministries in the community

Peacemaking

Mission service empowerment—solidarity with others: the poor and marginalized

Copier repair

Proper techniques for carving a hot for a hog roast

How to start the furnace

Communication: we are in time of global communication and we need as minister to study, explore, theologize about communication, we have to redefine the mission in the communicational frame

Multicultural formation: students have to be prepared to be ministers in multicultural environment. Seminaries have to teach as a basic requirement other languages than Hebrew and Greek related with the context of each student.

Theology: students receive thousands of texts and books with theological content made by scholars and classic authors but do not have much time and motivation to produce theology according to their own context and experience

Socio-political tools: the students need more interaction between social, political, economical context and theological exercise. Seminaries have to be more concerned about the social, political, and economical issues and the relation of these issues with the theological productions

Management: many students will be pastors after graduation and management (conflict, administration, fund raising, etc.) are issues that seminaries do not emphasize

Intercultural worship and liturgy: seminary needs to encourage and train students to produce liturgical resources in a multicultural way to provide opportunity for their own congregation to produce liturgical resources according to their cultural context and Reformed theology

Pre-marriage counseling training

Blended families course

Funeral worship

Wedding worship

Capital campaigns

Stewardship campaigns

Music ministry

Stephen's ministry

Sermon series

Celebrating the liturgical calendar

Many things we have learnt from seminary are geared towards being a solo and senior pastor, so what about courses that teach us how to be an associate and apply other area of ministries we have learned from seminary

How to say no and mean it

How to run stewardship campaign

How to work with social services in the community

How to do a stewardship campaign

Intergenerational issues (older and younger members—ways to converse, learn, deal conflict)

Healthy guidelines for office hours, vacation/sick time, availability and educating your congregation about this

Sabbath-keeping and family as first priority

Learning to read and understand the congregations' context and personality

Staff-building

Boundaries for solo pastorate (or yoked)

Uniqueness of small churches

Training others in pastoral care

Maintaining personal spirituality

The things I've needed that seminary didn't provide have been provided by God's grace. For seminary to try to provide those things would just add another book rather than Platonic conversations, rest, or incubation. While we cannot say that "this" or "that" is what a pastor should be, but I think that seminary presidents should guide students in expectations – what is expected of them. Schools should look at good health – food, bed, heat, etc.—as a standard rather than something a student should have to hunt down. If the staff is not willing to eat the everyday fare of the students because of its effect on the body (see 'Supersize Me" film), then that food should not be served to the students. Not another book on self-care, but modeling.

TAXES! (I nearly went bankrupt my first year)—what's clergy tax, what's Social Security offset! Seminary told me that tax issues were only Presbytery's responsibility and Presbytery told me it was seminary's responsibility.

How to find resources—denominational, internet, other denominations

Robert's Rules/Parliamentary procedures (for session and presbytery)

Conflict resolution

Systems Theory

Personal boundaries/appropriate relationships

Ways to connect with other 1st call folks—though seminary, denominations, other

Expense sheets/tracking models

Spiritual practices for meetings

All kinds of prayer resources

Running a session meeting

How to manage a capital campaign

Need to and personal resources for personal Sabbath

Acknowledgment of what a privilege it is to share the most holy moments in people's lives—death, birth, crisis, etc.

Conflict management with volunteer and paid staff

Negotiating terms of call

Knowing when it's time to move on

Tools and resources for long-range planning

How to help a congregation discern God's call

Budgets, stewardship, fundraising

To work in a multicultural world and churches

To preach

To work with youth

Training elders and deacons

Planning processes

How to evangelize and to reach people from community near to church

Financial training

Creative liturgy

To deal with change in churches (to help churches to change and those who resist to change)

How to create liturgical symbols

Prayer—especially spontaneous prayer. In ministry, scrambling for authentic words happens almost daily

Trusting God. In seminary, it's a theological discussion. In ministry, it's as essential as breathing

Time management. We talked a lot about this, but actually doing it is nothing like what we talked about. I don't really have time for it.

Stealing material from other ministers—keep a notebook of good material, even give other ministers credit. But regardless, rely on others' ideas.

Parliamentary procedure—in any given situation. I'm expected to know Robert's Rules or procedure—I do not even own a copy!

Be ready to go public. Despite my insistence—to the contrary, I am still a minister while cutting my grass and driving through town. I am a quasi-celebrity in every restaurant in town.

People are most important – not Greek or Hebrew. Not John Calvin. Not even preaching. Caring for people is the most important task of ministry.

Reading. I read more the first month of seminary than I have in the last sixteen months. As a minister, you have to make time to read, or quickly, you run out of things to say.

Trust people—after all, it is their church, you are just the minister

Be ready for anything—missing offering plates, absent nursery workers, copier malfunctions, rotten garbage, van trouble, late night calls to unlock doors, absent teachers, missing notes, missing scripts, angry mothers, PowerPoint disasters, broken elevators, leaky roofs, sinking offices, and a playground covered in raw sewage. All of that happened this past May.

Things I still need to know—not necessarily seminary's responsibility:

How to manage committees
How to handle budgets
Coming up with stewardship ideas
How long do you counsel before recommending a professional
How to incorporate broken families into a traditional family role model church life
How to welcome and integrate new members
How to manage staff
When to make changes in worship
How to know when to begin a Building plan
How to plan to say good-bye when you say hello.

A plan before leaving seminary for continued support

Spiritual formation of church leaders

Pastoral vulnerability and healthy boundaries

Systems theory

Administrative leadership

Receiving the gifts of a parish in pastoral formation

Navigating church finances

How to shovel snow and fix toilets

Ethics of friendships in congregations and small communities

Teaching and preaching stewardship

Appendix II

In addition to the Bible, these are books (religious or secular) that we have found helpful in our ministries

Craig Barnes

Karl Barth, Church Dogmatics IV:I
Dietrich Bonhoeffer, *Life Together*
Graham Greene, *The Power and the Glory*
Marilynne Robinson, Gilead
Alexander Schmemann, *For the Life of the World*

Heidi Worthen Gamble

Dietrich Bonhoeffer, *The Cost of Discipleship*
Annie Dillard, *Teaching a Stone to Talk*
Ariel Gore, *The Mother Trip: Hip Mama's Guide to Staying Sane in the Chaos of Motherhood*
Anne Lamott, *Traveling Mercies: Some Thoughts on Faith*
Henri Nouwen, *Creative Ministry*

John T. Galloway

Doris Kearns Goodwin, *Team of Rivals*
David Gregory, *Dinner with a Perfect Stranger*
Jeffrey Marx, *Season of Life*
David Murrow, *Why Men Hate Going to Church*
Barbara Brown Taylor, *Leaving Church*

Thomas W. Gillespie

Karl Barth, *Evangelical Theology*
H. Grady David, *Design for Preaching*
Larry W. Hurtado, *Lord Jesus Christ*
John A. Mackay, *God's Order* (The Letter to the Ephesians)
Michael Polanyi, *Personal Knowledge*

Jud Hendrix

Diana Butler Bass, *The Practicing Congregation*

Frederick Buechner, *Godric*

James Fowler, *The Stages of Faith*

David Hawkins, *Transcending the Levels of Consciousness*

Ken Wilber, *No Boundaries*

Deborah van deusen Hunsinger

David Augsburger, *Helping People Forgive*

David Augsburger, *Hate Work*

Karl Barth, *Church Dogmatics, III/2*

Edwin Friedman, *Generation to Generation*

Marshall Rosenberg, *Nonviolent Communication: A Language of Life*

Elizabeth "Liz" Kaznak

Marjory Zoet Bankson, *The Call to the Soul, Six Stages of Spiritual Development*

Cheryl H. Keen, James P. Keen, Sharon Daloz Parks, and Laurent A. Daloz, *Common Fire: Lives of Commitment in a Complex World*

Sharon Daloz Parks, *Big Questions, Worthy Dreams: Mentoring Young Adults in their Search for Meaning, Purpose, & Faith*

Loughlan Sofield, Rosine Hammett and Carroll Juliano, *Building Community*

Sir John Templeton, *Wisdom from the World Religions, Pathways toward Heaven on Earth*

Hope Lee

Donald Miller, *Blue Like Jazz: Non-Religious Thoughts on Christian Spirituality*

Sharon Daloz Parks, *Big Questions, Worthy Dreams: Mentoring Young Adults in their Search for Meaning, Purpose, & Faith*

Eugene Peterson, *Working the Angles: The Shape of Pastoral Integrity*

Haddon Robinson, *Biblical Preaching: The Development & Delivery of Expository Messages*

Mike Yaconelli, *Messy Spirituality: God's Annoying Love for Imperfect People*

Sung Lee

Dietrich Bonhoeffer, *The Cost of Discipleship*

Darrell L. Guder (editor), *Missional Church: A Vision for the Sending of the Church in North America*

C.S. Lewis, *Mere Christianity*

Michael Yaconelli, *Dangerous Wonder*

Michael Yaconelli, *Messy Spirituality: God's Annoying Love for Imperfect People*

Lonnie Oliver

Yosef ben-Jochannon, *African Origins of the Major Western Religions*

Howard L. Rice, *Reformed Spirituality*

Donald A. Smith, *Empowering Ministry: Ways to Grow in Effectiveness*

Cornell West, *Race Matters*

Gayraud S. Wilmore, *Pragmatic Spirituality*

Neal D. Presa

Frederick Buechner, *Telling the Truth: The Gospel as Tragedy, Comedy, and Fairy Tale*

Gordon Lathrop, *Holy Things: A Liturgical Theology*

Richard Lischer, *Open Secrets: A Spiritual Journey Through a Country Church*

Henri Nouwen, *Wounded Healer*

J.I. Packer, *Knowing God*

Bruce Reyes-Chow

Sherry Ruth Anderson and Paul H. Ray, *The Cultural Creative*

David Brooks, *Bobos in Paradise*

Richard Florida, *The Rise of the Creative Class*

Brian McLaren, *A Generous Orthodoxy*

James K.A. Smith, *Who's Afraid of Postmodernism*

David Shinn

Thomas Edward Frank, *The Soul of the Congregation*

Anne Lamott, *Bird by Bird*

Ted Loder, *My Heart in My Mouth*

Thomas Long, *Testimony: Talking Ourselves into being Christian*

Robin Meyers, *Why the Christian Right is Wrong*

Henri Nouwen, *Life of the Beloved*

Mienda Uriarte

David Brooks, *On Paradise Drive*

Michael O. Emerson and Rodney Woo, *People of the Dream: Multiracial Congregations in the United States*

John P. Kotter, *Leading Change*

Jung Young Lee, *Marginality: The Key to Multicultural Theology*

Everett M. Rogers, *Diffusion of Innovation*

Steve Yamaguchi

Chris Argyris, *Reasons and Rationalizations: The Limits to Organizational Knowledge*

Shusaku Endo, *Silence (Chinmoku)*

Thomas L. Friedman, *The World is Flat*

Martin Hengel, *Crucifixion in the Ancient World and the Folly of the Message of the Cross*

Lesslie Newbigin, *A Word in Season: Perspectives on Christian World Missions*

About the Editor

Neal D. Presa is pastor of Middlesex Presbyterian Church, Middlesex, NJ and a PhD candidate in liturgical studies at Drew University. He is also a Henry Luce Foundation Graduate Fellow with the Center for Christianities in Global Context at Drew University. Neal represents the Presbyterian Church (U.S.A.) as the Convenor/Chair of the Caribbean and North American Area Council of the World Alliance of Reformed Churches (WARC), and on the WARC Executive Committee. He has served at every level of the Presbyterian Church (U.S.A.) including the Committee on Theological Education, Vice Chair of the General Assembly Council, the Committee on the Office of the General Assembly, Presbytery Council, and the Committee on Preparation for Ministry. He received his BA from University of California (Davis), graduate studies at Westminister Theological Seminary in CA, MDiv from San Francisco Theological Seminary and a ThM from Princeton Theological Seminary.

He has written articles in *Call to Worship, Homily Service* journal, *The Presbyterian Outlook, These Days, and The Present Word.*

He enjoys movie nights and traveling with his wife and two sons.

Printed in the United States
201355BV00001B/1-105/P

9 781565 913578